GLOBAL ORGANIZATIONS

The United Nations Children's Fund

GLOBAL ORGANIZATIONS

The African Union

The Arab League

The Association of Southeast Asian Nations

The Caribbean Community

The European Union

The International Atomic Energy Agency

The Organization of American States

The Organization of the Petroleum
Exporting Countries

The United Nations

The United Nations Children's Fund

The World Bank and
the International Monetary Fund

The World Health Organization

The World Trade Organization

GLOBAL ORGANIZATIONS

The United Nations Children's Fund

Ada Verloren

Series Editor
Peggy Kahn
University of Michigan–Flint

CHELSEA HOUSE
PUBLISHERS
An imprint of Infobase Publishing

Chelsea House
An imprint of Infobase Publishing
132 West 31st Street
New York NY 10001

Library of Congress Cataloging-in-Publication Data
Verloren, Ada.
The United Nations Children's Fund / by Ada Verloren.
    p. cm. — (Global organizations)
Includes bibliographical references and index.
ISBN 978-0-7910-9566-9 (hardcover)
1. UNICEF. 2. Child welfare. 3. Child welfare—Haiti. 4. Children's rights. I. Title.

HV703.V47 2009
362.7—dc22   2008055364

Chelsea House books are available at special discounts when purchased in bulk quantities for businesses, associations, institutions, or sales promotions. Please call our Special Sales Department in New York at (212) 967-8800 or (800) 322-8755.

You can find Chelsea House on the World Wide Web at http://www.chelseahouse.com

Series design by Erik Lindstrom
Cover design by Ben Peterson

Printed in the United States of America

Bang KT 10 9 8 7 6 5 4 3 2 1

This book is printed on acid-free paper.

All links and Web addresses were checked and verified to be correct at the time of publication. Because of the dynamic nature of the Web, some addresses and links may have changed since publication and may no longer be valid.

CONTENTS

INTRODUCTION

Help for Haiti

Lord be merciful to us, we shall be all lost, we shall be all undone ... such a dismal Sight I never saw: The Sea went Mountains high, and broke upon us every three or four Minutes: when I could look about, I could see nothing but Distress round us. ...[1]

—Daniel Defoe, *Robinson Crusoe*

THE PEOPLE OF HAITI WERE ALREADY LIVING WITH BARE cupboards and empty stomachs when, in August and September 2008, a series of powerful storms and hurricanes cut a path of destruction across their island nation, the poorest in the Western Hemisphere. Almost like curses, tropical storms Fay and Hanna, and hurricanes Gustav and Ike relentlessly blasted hurricane-force winds and dumped seemingly endless rains on this struggling country. Four heavy storms in less than a month killed more than 800 and left tens of thousands injured and homeless in Haiti.

On August 15, the furious Fay drenched Haiti and flooded rice fields. Soon after, forecasters predicted that Gustav's winds would reach speeds of 111 miles per hour. Prompted by hurricane warnings, Haitians started to brace themselves for more flooding and damage. Barely a week later, Hanna flooded the seaside city of Gonaïves and stranded tens of thousands of people. More than 10,000 people fled the city, walking, wading, and swimming toward the next town, about 45 miles to the south. Aid workers handed out food and water to the famished Haitians who remained in Gonaïves. The floodwaters took at least 163 lives. Within a few days, at least 58 more people drowned as Ike passed through the beleaguered island and generated large swells at sea. With winds up to 135 miles per hour, rains came down horizontally. Floods rushed down mountains that had been stripped long ago of trees for use as fuel. Rivers broke their banks. Floodwater isolated the hungry and suffering people in Gonaïves. "What I saw in this city today is close to hell on earth," worried Hédi Annabi, the United Nations special representative to Haiti.[2]

These devastating storms thrashed agricultural lands, killed farm animals, and washed away small stores of food. Survivors in the city of Gonaïves, who had possessed very little before the storms, now had nothing. Humble homes were underwater. School was canceled. Floodwater covered the city's hospital. Hunger was extreme. Desperate children and adults urgently sought food and clean water. As the floods receded, residents struggled along roads covered with a heavy, brown, foul mix of water and mud reaching their ankles, their knees, or sometimes even their hips.

It was an enormous calamity and the United Nations Children's Fund (UNICEF) prepared to deal with it. After tropical storm Hanna flooded Gonaïves, UNICEF, together with

Over a three-week period in August 2008, four powerful storms pounded Haiti, affecting some 800,000 people, including at least 300,000 children. In Haiti, one of the world's poorest countries, storms can devastate entire communities due to poorly constructed homes, massive deforestation, and the government's lack of an evacuation plan or shelter system. UNICEF and the World Food Program provided food, water, purification tablets, blankets, and other relief supplies, and made more than $1 million available to help hurricane victims.

the World Food Program, was ready to transport tons of food and thousands of gallons of water to the affected nation. Access to the city was next to impossible: roads were flooded, and bad weather conditions made access by sea or air very difficult.

At Jubilee National School, two-year-old Fernando Thermidor buried his tear-stained face in his mother's shoulder. Along with nearly 200 other people, Fernando, his mother, Judith, and the rest of the family of five, were crammed into a classroom. "We have been sleeping here—the whole family—for the past week. We had to run out of our house with only the clothes on our backs when the water rose," said Judith.[3]

A piercing shout at the shelter announced the arrival of the truck with safe water from UNICEF and food from the World Food Program. This life-sustaining aid finally reached the area by helicopter and boat. Many more tons of emergency aid was already under way from UNICEF's supply headquarters in Copenhagen, Denmark: eleven and a half tons of blankets, hygiene kits, water purification tablets, and oral rehydration salts for treating dehydration from diarrhea. The load also included School-in-a-Box kits including books, pencils, colored pencils, erasers, notepads, chalks, slates, and a bag. Although an ideal shopping list probably would have included items like a laptop, a calculator, or air-conditioning, UNICEF still provided some of the most essential materials to help children return to school when their lives once again became normal.

The start date for the school year was delayed for a month, until October 6. Because all of the schools in the disaster zone were being used as shelters, the first challenge was to relocate thousands of families and to make the school structures safe and sanitary for students. UNICEF Goodwill Ambassador and actor Mia Farrow described the magnitude of this challenge when she said, "All over town, it's like a big 'SOS.'"[4] Students helping to clean mud out of school buildings were daunted by the enormity of the task. "I look at all this dirt and trash and I wonder when can school start?" said Sanon Verlaine, 18, as he looked at a schoolyard littered with trash and debris. UNICEF was working closely with the Ministry of Education to determine which schools could reopen soon and which schools would have to resume in temporary settings.[5]

Although the floodwaters receded and buildings were free from mud, UNICEF continues to assist Haitians with the enormous challenges that they face. Even when not complicated by a natural disaster, providing education for Haitian children has been difficult. Only about 50 percent of school-age children attend primary school, and only 2 percent complete their secondary education. UNICEF has helped communities build new schools and has provided water and sanitation supplies.

Almost 60 percent of Haitians, especially those living in rural areas, do not have access to basic health-care services. With supplies, medical equipment, and assistance from UNICEF workers, more children have been immunized. Haiti has been free of measles and polio since 2001.

UNICEF's initial task after World War II was to assist children in emergencies such as war, ethnic conflict, or other crises. While its work has shifted to protecting more broadly the rights of children, especially in developing countries, UNICEF still aids in emergencies. When UNICEF responds to a natural disaster, it is guided by the principle that these children have the same needs and rights as children in stable situations. In crises, malnutrition and illnesses such as diarrhea and acute respiratory infections are real threats to children's lives. Therefore UNICEF's priorities are emergency immunizations, good nutrition, clean water, and sanitation. It also focuses on protecting children from violence and reintegrating them into their communities. UNICEF also supports education programs to bring children back to schools where they can find the stability and security that is necessary for healthy development.

UNICEF leads the worldwide campaign to respect children's rights and to meet their needs, both in emergencies and in their daily lives. While UNICEF cannot stop storms and hurricanes from crossing the oceans, it can relieve some of the misery they cause. In the aftermath of such emergencies, UNICEF embodies the hope that attention to children's health and welfare today will lead to a world that is truly fit for children.

Improving the Lives of Children

For every child
Health, Education, Equality, Protection
ADVANCE HUMANITY
—UNICEF slogan[6]

WHY DO CHILDREN NEED SPECIAL PROTECTION? ONE OF THE most direct and undeniable answers to this question is one that U.S. president Herbert Hoover gave after he toured 38 countries in 1946, after two devastating wars were fought in Europe. On the radio, at press conferences, and in front of live audiences, Hoover called for a full-blown campaign against child hunger and malnutrition. He stated his reasons starkly and urgently: "From the Russian frontier to the Channel, there are today twenty millions of children who are not only badly undernourished, but steadily developing tuberculosis, rickets, and anemia. If Europe is to have a future, something must be done about these children."[7] Today, children on other continents still need special protection or help for similar reasons; if every continent is to have a future, something must be done about its children.

LIFE IN KIBERA

Children need many kinds of help. Fourteen-year-old Maureen grew up poor in Kibera, a sprawling slum area in Nairobi, Kenya, in Africa, which is home to over 800,000 people. Violence, burglary, and disease are common in her neighborhood, where almost nobody has running water or electricity.

Maureen is a bright student, at the top of her class in math and English. Although she dreams of becoming an accountant, her dreams almost ended when she lost both her parents to AIDS. She moved in with her aunt and had to stop going to school for a year because her aunt could not afford to pay the school fees.

Maureen was able to go back to school only after the Kenyan government eliminated the school fees. UNICEF made the difference, donating funds for materials, for makeshift classrooms, and for training teachers. Grants and other support also came from international organizations such as the World Bank and the World Food Program.[8]

Because Maureen's school is located in a densely populated slum area, contaminated water and inadequate sanitation systems present her with serious health risks. With support from UNICEF's country office in Kenya, the school has installed toilets for boys and girls as well as three large cisterns (large storage tanks that hold rain water) to increase the school's supply of clean water. Maureen and other children have joined the WASH-in-Schools Initiative, a project of Water Advocates, a global voluntary coalition of governmental

UNICEF works to ensure that every child has access to a quality education, regardless of gender, ethnicity, or socioeconomic status. With a broad range of local and international partners, they have built schools, trained teachers, and even rebuilt entire educational systems. Above, Sudanese children attend a UNICEF-sponsored school in the Farshana refugee camp in eastern Chad.

and nongovernmental organizations (NGOs) that promotes hand-washing and pushes for wide access to water in poor areas. Through the WASH program, these students are responsible for cleaning and maintaining the bathroom facilities in their schools and homes. They also educate other children and their communities about cleanliness, an important way to decrease the danger of contracting diseases.

Health care is an ongoing concern in Maureen's community, where many persons suffer from HIV/AIDS and other infectious diseases. Mobile clinics, operated by a nongovernmental organization, provide immunizations and other health services. In addition, UNICEF coordinates vaccination campaigns against such diseases as measles and tetanus. Unfortunately, there is no vaccine yet against malaria, a real danger to Maureen and other children; still, the Kenyan government, UNICEF, and private corporations have joined together to campaign against the conditions that promote malaria.

Maureen has been fortunate to avoid the violence that has ravaged many of her friends' lives both at home and in school. In 2001, the government of Kenya enacted the Children's Act, which forbids corporal punishment and all forms of child labor that are exploitative, although the government is not always able to effectively enforce the law. In 2007, UNICEF's Goodwill Ambassador for Eastern and Southern Africa, South African hip-hop star Zola, visited schools in Kenya to meet with children and urged communities to stop the cycle of violence.

Children are not incapable and helpless. Many often show that they can develop strategies to cope with impossible hardship. Still, Maureen and other children need care and protection because they are young and have less power than adults to shape their everyday lives and to take care of themselves. All people have rights or entitlements just because they are human and deserving of the right to live a healthy and safe life; the right to receive an education; and the right to be protected from abuse, exploitation, and violence. Children cannot protect their own rights themselves, so it is everyone's job to work to make human rights real.

CREATION OF NGOs AND IGOs

Who protects children and takes care of them? Caregivers include family members, governments, international organizations, private corporations, and NGOs, as well as volunteers, dedicated individuals, and children's peers. Many people would say that parents and relatives have the main responsibility because they are usually responsible for daily care of the child: feeding, bathing, and taking care of his or her health, protection, and emotional care. Many believe that the local community and government, however, also are responsible for a child's care. During the late twentieth and early twenty-first centuries, national and local governments have ensured that a child's most basic needs are met—that every child receives nutrition, education, health care, and protection from violence, exploitation, and discrimination.

Before the early twentieth century, families and nations were not always able to care for and protect children, especially during wars and conflicts. Individuals and governments joined together to create international organizations to perform these tasks. Some of these were NGOs, which have no connection to governments, like the Save the Children Fund. Others were intergovernmental organizations (IGOs), in which several governments work together to fulfill a need and to carry out mutual needs in a unified form. The most prominent of the IGOs is the United Nations (UN), created in 1945 after World War II by representatives from 51 countries who wanted to prevent conflicts between nations and to make future wars impossible.

THE UNICEF STRUCTURE

The United Nations system is comprised of the UN itself and more than 30 affiliated organizations. These affiliates are programs, funds, or specialized agencies, including UNICEF. As one of the UN programs and funds, UNICEF has its own leadership, membership, and budget processes. It finances its work entirely through voluntary contributions from governments, foundations, UN agencies, international financial institutions, individuals, and businesses.

Thirty-six national committees play a large role in raising funds, up to one-third of UNICEF's resources. Although these committees do not deliver services or make policies, they raise funds on behalf of the entire international organization, not just for work within their own countries. National committees, such as the United States Committee, also educate the public and make the organization more visible through a variety of campaigns. One such campaign, called Trick-or-Treat for UNICEF, involves children going door-to-door on Halloween to collect donations. Since October 31, 1950, when a handful of children in Philadelphia collected $17 for UNICEF, children have raised more than $132 million to save and improve lives of children around the world.[9]

UNICEF has a presence in more than 190 countries and territories. More than 120 country offices work with host governments to develop five-year plans focusing on practical ways to realize the rights of children and women. Seven regional offices guide the work of the country offices and provide technical assistance as needed.

Specialized offices include the Supply Division, which is based in Copenhagen, Denmark, and is the main point of distribution, providing essential items such as vaccines for children in developing countries. The scale of this work is enormous. For example, polio eradication efforts alone require purchasing and distributing up to 2.3 billion doses of oral polio vaccine in one year.[10] UNICEF also operates the Innocenti Research Center in Florence, Italy, to strengthen the research capabilities

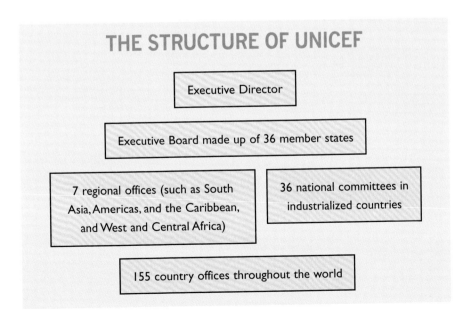

THE STRUCTURE OF UNICEF

Executive Director

Executive Board made up of 36 member states

7 regional offices (such as South Asia, Americas, and the Caribbean, and West and Central Africa)

36 national committees in industrialized countries

155 country offices throughout the world

of UNICEF and to promote the effective implementation of the Convention on the Rights of the Child.

Because UNICEF is a field-based organization delivering services "on the ground" such as health services, support for schools, and protective services for children who are at risk of being abused, it has a large staff working in 155 different countries. By contrast, overall management and administration of the organization takes place at its relatively small headquarters in New York.

At UNICEF's head is the executive director, who is appointed for a 10-year term by the UN secretary general. The post traditionally has gone to an American since the United States played an important role in creating the agency following WWII. The United States continues to provide strong financial support for UNICEF, but there has been public criticism in regards to what others perceive as the influence of powerful countries like the United States to make political appointments to important posts.[11]

In 2005, Ann M. Veneman was appointed as the fifth executive director of UNICEF. An attorney and former U.S. Secretary of Agriculture, Veneman grew up on a family farm in California's Central Valley. As the first woman at the helm of the United States Department of Agriculture, she focused her attention on helping to feed the hungry around the world. She supported good nutrition for children through school lunch and breakfast programs, and she sought to protect public health through safe food supplies. In her current role, Ms. Veneman visits many parts of the world, drawing attention to the plight of children and women, and meeting with presidents, private corporations, NGOs, and international organizations to build partnerships and to bring improvements in areas such as health and education. "Children are the future," Ms. Veneman said on a recent visit to Swaziland. "They are the future of every country; they're the future of everything

Since assuming her position in 2005, Executive Director Ann Veneman has made achieving the UN Millennium Development Goals a priority because of their focus on helping the world's children. The *Lancet* medical journal praised her vision, stating that she "has pledged the agency to what amounts to a second child survival revolution." Here, Veneman poses with school children during a visit to the Dvumbe Primary School, near Mbabane, Swaziland, in Africa.

this world is going to be about, and so anything that we can do to better the world for children will benefit humankind."[12]

The executive director works closely with a 36-member executive board, which guides and monitors UNICEF's work. Board members represent governments from Africa (8), Asia (7), Eastern Europe (4), Latin America and the Caribbean (5), and Western Europe and other states (12). Together they formulate policies, authorize programs, and approve financial plans and budgets.

As a member of the UN family, UNICEF and other groups work with and through the UN to promote worldwide peace and stability. UNICEF has had effective partnerships with other UN specialized agencies, such as the World Health Organization (WHO), a specialized international agency setting health policy and advising countries' governments with regard to health initiatives. UNICEF helped with its work on the Roll Back Malaria campaign.

UNICEF's "extended family" reaches beyond the UN to include NGOs closely associated with the agency's work, from large networks, such as the Save the Children Alliance, to small village water committees. Besides giving information and advice, NGOs help to implement UNICEF's programs throughout the world, like providing food and supplies in emergencies, building primary schools, supplying safe water and sanitation, and immunizing children.

UNICEF's work is further enhanced by partnerships with corporations and businesses, which support UNICEF's programs and emergency relief efforts. Support comes in the form of grants, contributions, or assistance. Some of these businesses are national companies operating within a single country, such as Botswana's primary mobile telephone company, Mascom, which has donated to orphan care projects. Others are multinational corporations, such as Scandinavian furniture and home goods store Ikea, which donated 9,000

THE UNICEF SYMBOL

UNICEF's goals are captured in its striking emblem, which is similar to the United Nations' emblem. Both have the globe surrounded by olive branches, symbolizing world peace. In the center of UNICEF's emblem is a mother holding a baby. This emblem signifies universal recognition that children are every nation's tomorrow and that children's survival, protection, and development are critical for a peaceful future. The emblem further recognizes the essential role of adults—in families, schools, and society in general—in nurturing children. UNICEF shares in this responsibility as it urgently works to improve the lives of children and their families.

The UNICEF logo outside of UNICEF Germany.

tables to support UNICEF's work in Liberia. Corporate partnerships have advantages for UNICEF as well as for the companies. Through partnering with UNICEF, companies strengthen their corporate image, demonstrate that they care about social conditions, and promote positive relations with their customers.

In addition to partnerships with UN specialized agencies, NGOs, and corporations, UNICEF benefits from the support of internationally known personalities. Named Goodwill Ambassadors, these singers, actors, and athletes use their fame to make more people aware of the needs of children and to raise funds for the organization. One Goodwill Ambassador, classical pianist Lang Lang, the "hottest artist on the classical music planet,"[13] has created an international foundation to encourage children's love of music. Roger Federer, another Goodwill Ambassador, is not only one of the all-time greatest tennis players, but has also raised and donated funds for destitute children in South Africa.

UNICEF traditionally has been a favored partner of governments of developing countries. While UNICEF recognizes that governments shoulder the main responsibility for children's welfare, governments usually have welcomed UNICEF's provision of supplies and equipment, funding, and advice. Much of UNICEF's work has involved activities that are not tied to politics. Instead, UNICEF focuses upon moral imperatives, such as ensuring child survival, or upon operational assistance, such as providing equipment and supplies like syringes and vaccines. Although governments have embraced UNICEF's assistance with tasks that would otherwise be neglected because of a lack of staff or resources, governments sometimes can be sensitive to criticism from international organizations.

Since the adoption of the Convention on the Rights of the Child in 1989, UNICEF sometimes has become a "critical partner" of governments accused of violating the rights of children. UNICEF has had to be careful not to openly criticize a government's policies and programs, since open criticism of a government may make it harder for UNICEF to work in that country. Instead, UNICEF consults quietly with governments, directs their attention to children's rights, and calls for changes to policies that do not respect these rights. UNICEF's role is to try to convince governments that they should change their laws and practices. UNICEF, in its role as an advocate for children's rights, emphasizes that investing in children's well-being and protecting their rights are necessary for development and social change. UNICEF sometimes influences governments by partnering with politicians, who have the power to create and enforce legislation that protects children and to make sure that funding is available to address children's needs.

UNICEF'S Five Areas of Focus are:

- *Child survival and development*: treatment of preventable diseases such as measles and malaria.
- *HIV/AIDS and children*: preventing the spread of the disease and supporting children whose lives have been impacted by HIV/AIDS, including AIDS orphans.
- *Basic education and gender equality*: ensuring that all children around the globe have access to education.
- *Child protection from violence, exploitation, and abuse*: shielding young people from child labor, armed conflict, and other harmful situations.
- *Policy advocacy and partnerships for children's rights*: working to keep the spotlight on the rights of children.

Progress in these five areas has been possible because of UNICEF's unique structure. UNICEF has an immediate connection to the highest corridors of power, while at the same time, it works with ordinary citizens who want to help children. At the highest level, UNICEF is part of the UN family and is closely connected to governments. The members of its executive board are government representatives who are also members of the United Nations, but UNICEF also has a grass-roots presence through the work of its field staff working on the ground in communities. UNICEF's national committees raise donations and apply pressure, from below, on government leaders. UNICEF also depends on partnerships with NGOs and corporations, and on the help of celebrities who serve as Goodwill Ambassadors. UNICEF has successfully marshaled the energy of volunteers, teenagers, and schoolchildren to work for the cause of children. UNICEF's achievements have depended on its ability to get the support from presidents and students, from sports stars and musicians, from doctors and local volunteers, who all share in humanity's desire to work for the cause of children.

UNICEF's path has not been easy. It was created "to work with others to overcome the obstacles that poverty, violence, disease, and discrimination place in a child's path"[14] and it is a seemingly uphill battle. Nearly 10 million children under the age of 5 die every year, many from preventable causes. HIV/AIDS continues to devastate communities. One child in six is severely hungry. One in seven receives no health care. More than one billion people do not have access to an uncontaminated water supply. Almost half of the world's population lives without basic sanitation. Over one million primary-school-age children do not attend school. Children are disproportionately affected by war and other disasters. On which challenge should UNICEF focus? Does it spend money and energy on responding to ever-present emergencies, such as a hurricane in Haiti or the conflict in Darfur? Does it help countries to achieve long-term development so that governments can improve the quality of life for children and their families? While UNICEF pays attention to all these challenges simultaneously, it sometimes has to make hard choices in setting priorities.

The History of UNICEF

Everyone has understood the language of UNICEF, and even the most reluctant person is bound to admit that in action UNICEF has proved that compassion knows no national boundaries. . . . The aid given must cover all children in an area, regardless of race, creed, nationality, or political conviction. . . . UNICEF offers young people in all countries an alternative worth living and working for, a world with freedom for all people, equality between all races. . . .[15]

—From Nobel Citation awarding UNICEF the Nobel Prize for Peace, December 10, 1965

A few days after his appointment as UNICEF's first executive director in January 1947, Maurice Pate wrote to the U.S. Secretary of State. The compassionate Pate, a former U.S.

government official with extensive experience doing humanitarian relief work in Belgium and Poland during two world wars, asked for $100 million "to provide a glass of milk and some fat to be spread on bread . . . for six million hungry children in Europe and China."[16] In the aftermath of World War II, millions of children who had unwillingly left their homes and the countries in which they were born found themselves without one or both parents, without a place to stay, without heating, without clothing, and without food. Deadly illnesses were spreading quickly and medical supplies were scarce. In this harsh environment, half of all European babies died before their first birthday.

"The food of many poor families is little more than watery soup, carried from a nearby kitchen. . . . In some parts of the country families are living on potatoes. The women walk miles each day, begging and foraging for food,"[17] said Pate. These distressing words described the pitiful condition of Polish children, but the misery of children was not confined to Poland. It extended from southern Italy to Germany, Ukraine, and many other parts of eastern and central Europe. Pale children with emaciated bodies lived in buildings partly destroyed by bombs or slept in soggy trenches during the terribly cold winter of 1946–1947. In southern Italy, homeless boys found temporary shelter in caves and roamed the streets in groups without supervision or support. In Czechoslovakia, children without shoes or winter coats suffered in freezing temperatures. In Germany, children played among the ruins of war and in the holes left by bombs. There was a dangerous food shortage everywhere. A severe drought, a shortage of seed, a lack of fertilizer, a scarcity of farm animals to help pull ploughs, and a dearth of other equipment hindered farmers' efforts to grow crops in battlefields overgrown with weeds.

This destruction caused by World War II spurred the global community into creating the United Nations International Children's Emergency Fund (UNICEF). Dr. Ludwig Rajchman, a Polish doctor, generally is regarded as the founder of UNICEF. He proposed that funds remaining from the United Nations Relief and Rehabilitation Agency (UNRRA), the major postwar relief program, be used for the emergency needs of European children, especially for controlling and preventing widespread disease. At the time, the world had no intention of creating a permanent organization for children, expecting that it only needed a short-term solution to a one-time emergency. By 1953, it became clear that, in addition to short-term emergencies, enduring poverty in Asia, Africa, and the Americas led to millions of children in distress. It was a turning point for UNICEF when that year it dropped the words *International* and *Emergency* from its name and became simply known as the United Nations Children's Fund, although it retained its well-known acronym, UNICEF. UNICEF changed from an emergency fund to a permanent development organization, one trying to improve basic conditions and quality of life for children in poor countries over the long run.

THE EMERGENCY RESPONSE: 1940s AND 1950s

In response to Pate's plea, an expert group of pediatricians and nutritionists recommended supplying animal protein, calcium, and vitamins to millions of starving children in Europe. Milk powder provided the best all-inclusive solution for undernourished children, with its nutritious blend of animal fat, protein, vitamins, and minerals. When the SS *Mark Hanna* docked at a Polish harbor from New York in 1947 with 450 tons of powered milk for the children of Poland, 800 enthusiastic children were there to greet the ship and to thank the donors: the United Nations, UNICEF, and the American people. After they sang songs, recited poems, and gave speeches, the children were invited to go on board the ship, where the captain and crew handed out rare treats, such as sweets and oranges.

Despite their enthusiastic welcome, children were hesitant to actually drink milk made from skim milk powder, which

Following the devastation of World War II, 20 million children were in desperate need of emergency assistance. Half of all babies were dying before their first birthday. In response, the UN General Assembly created UNICEF in 1946. By 1948, the organization was providing food and other items to 5 million children in 12 countries. Above, in 1948, a worker distributed food at the UNICEF mission in Austria.

smelled and tasted bad. Mothers, teachers, and nurses distributing milk at feeding centers had to discover ways to make the milk seem more appealing. Hot milk tasted better than cold; sugar made it taste even better; and adding noodles or macaroni helped to improve the flavor. Gradually, in addition to supplying European countries with milk powder, UNICEF also helped with the recovery of Europe's dairy industry so that countries eventually were able to produce safe, pasteurized milk for children. UNICEF became known as "the cup of milk organization" and the "milkman of the world's children." It was only in 1960 that the now familiar mother and child symbol replaced the old UNICEF emblem of a child with a cup of milk.

The size of UNICEF's relief operation was staggering. Between 1947 and 1951, it shipped more than 400 million pounds of milk powder, enough to make 6.4 billion cups of milk and to feed 7 million infants and children. The International Tuberculosis Campaign, taking place around that time, reached even more children.[18] UNICEF supplied jeeps, trucks, needles, vaccines, and syringes to Scandinavian teams of nurses and doctors who vaccinated children against tuberculosis all across Europe. The campaign later branched out across Africa, Asia, and Latin America. When it ended in 1951, it had tested 30 million children and had vaccinated 14 million children in 23 countries.[19]

Mass campaigns to eradicate disease were not always successful. One failure was the fight against malaria. Launched in 1955 by UNICEF and the World Health Organization (WHO), the campaign initially promised to eliminate all malaria-carrying mosquitoes by widespread spraying of the pesticide DDT (dichloro-diphenyl-trichloroethane). UNICEF supplied DDT and spraying equipment, but it did not have enough funding to apply DDT in every corner of the world. As a result, some malarial mosquitoes developed a resistance to DDT, and others avoided landing on areas sprayed with the poison. In addition, the fight against malaria campaign was abolished after protests by environmental groups brought awareness of the long-lasting poison's potential damage to the planet.

Malaria continues to be a life-threatening disease, especially to people living in rural areas in developing countries who do not have access to anti-malarial drugs. Recent attempts to eradicate malaria have focused on making available insecticide-treated bed nets. A vaccine has yet to be developed.

THE DEVELOPMENT DECADES: 1960s–1980s

In January 1961, the UN General Assembly designated the 1960s as the first UN Development Decade. This decade recognized the changes occurring within many countries that had recently broken free of their colonial status. In 1960 alone, 17 former African colonies declared independence from their colonial rulers. Independence created excitement and hope; it also caused concern about the grinding poverty of many people in the newly independent nations. The world admitted that it was morally unacceptable that some people lived well, while others lived in extreme poverty. To change the situation, richer countries would have to assist developing countries by providing funds and technical expertise. The concept of "development" implied that developing countries would cast off their poverty and over time create a higher standard of living and improved well-being for their people. Development also signified, on a more humane level, an awareness that persons mattered and that the well-being of every person, rich or poor, was of utmost importance.

To define its role in development, UNICEF initiated a special survey of the basic needs of children. The final report, *Children of the Developing Countries*, outlined the importance of fulfilling children's needs as countries were designing development plans. UNICEF realized that it could no longer only consider children's physical well-being and health, but that it had to take into account the "whole child." As a result, UNICEF began to address children's intellectual, psychological, and social needs. In addition to its work in traditional areas such as food and health care, UNICEF started providing water and sanitation. It paid special attention to the many ways in which girls suffered discrimination. For example, girls, unlike boys, often were not allowed to attend school, and even if they were, their opinions were not respected. Many girls were forced to marry at a young age, and many girls suffered sexual exploitation. Now, for the first time, UNICEF was willing to provide funds for education.

UNICEF's main concern was that development should result in real and concrete benefits for poor children. Yet, despite growth in the economies of developing countries, there was often little or no improvement in the lives of the poor. The failure of development to end serious poverty was partly due to a rapid increase in developing countries' populations. Not only were people living longer, but there were also more births and more children surviving into adulthood than in the past. Development also failed to reach many poor people because existing services, such as health care or education, rarely reached small villages. And even if the services did extend to remote places, they did not necessarily address needs that villagers identified as important.

To meet basic needs, especially of those people living far away from urban centers, UNICEF's solution was to train "barefoot" workers to deliver local services. Barefoot workers are ordinary members of a community who volunteer to perform simple tasks such as weighing babies, taking care of and stimulating young children, and maintaining hand pumps to supply safe water. Having volunteers perform these routine activities under professional supervision reduced the need for paid workers not familiar with the region to perform these services. With the help of barefoot workers, services could reach more people without raising the cost.

UNICEF continued to provide emergency relief during unusual catastrophes. One such catastrophe was the Nigerian civil war of 1967–1970. Nigerian government forces prevented anybody from entering or leaving the breakaway "republic" of Biafra in southeast Nigeria, starving many of its inhabitants. Although the government would not give permission for the UN to help the famished Biafran children, it made an exception for UNICEF on the basis of its record of helping children on both sides of a conflict. UNICEF's neutrality in the conflict allowed it to get food and other supplies to the starving Biafran population.

The 1970s ended with the UN's declaration of 1979 as the International Year of the Child. UNICEF, initially reluctant to

WINNING THE NOBEL PEACE PRIZE

In 1965, UNICEF was awarded the Nobel Prize for Peace in recognition of its work on behalf of victims of armed conflict. During UNICEF's first field operations in Europe after WWII, it contended that no child was an "enemy child." During the 1960s, when UNICEF took up the enormous task of improving the miserable conditions of children living in developing countries, it aided all children regardless of race, creed, nationality, or political conviction. With its actions, UNICEF helped to establish the idea that mutual help between people, and between rich and poor nations, was necessary to raise the standard of living everywhere.

In accepting the Nobel Prize, Henry R. Labouisse, Executive Director of UNICEF, explained that the biggest threat to peace was the "slow war of attrition which poverty and ignorance now wage against 800 million children in the developing countries."[*] The Nobel Prize reinforced UNICEF's belief that each time it contributes "to giving today's children a chance to grow into useful and happier citizens, it contributes to removing some of the seeds of world tension and future conflicts."[**]

---

[*] "Acceptance speech by Henry R. Labouisse, Executive Director of UNICEF, on the occasion of the award of the Nobel Peace Prize in Oslo, December 10, 1965." Available online at http://nobelprize.org/nobel_prizes/peace/laureates/1965/unicef-acceptance.html.

[**] Ibid.

participate in an event that might not yield concrete benefits for children, eventually played a leading role in this remarkably successful event. The International Year of the Child was an opportunity to celebrate, recognize, and praise the efforts of everybody who took care of children. It also drew UNICEF's attention to a group who had not received previous special attention—street children. In addition, UNICEF came to realize that it was not enough to focus on children in developing countries; in industrialized countries many children also went without protection, without education, and without health care.

GOBI

The success of the 1979 International Year of the Child gave UNICEF a sense of purpose to deal with the challenges of the 1980s, the third UN Development Decade. The biggest and most basic challenge was to ensure child survival. To directly attack infant and child mortality, the tirelessly energetic and resourceful James P. Grant, UNICEF's new executive director, started an initiative known as "the child survival revolution." It focused on four practices that became known as GOBI:

G stands for growth monitoring to make sure that every child has enough food and is growing at a healthy pace;

O is for oral rehydration therapy to deal with childhood diarrhea;

B is for breastfeeding as the perfect way to feed newborn babies;

I is for immunization against six potentially deadly childhood diseases—tuberculosis, diphtheria, whooping cough, tetanus, polio, and measles.

These low-cost techniques contributed to putting "children first." Inspired by this saying, Grant traveled across the world, carrying around a packet of oral rehydration salts, a mixture of salt and glucose in the correct proportions. When he encountered a mother with a sick baby, he would show her how to mix the salts with water to save the life of a child with diarrhea. The esteemed medical journal *The Lancet* called oral rehydration therapy "potentially the most important medical advance of this century."[20]

The benefits of immunization had become so well known and widely accepted that even combatants in war were willing to temporarily stop fighting so that children could be vaccinated. In 1985, during the bitter civil war in El Salvador, conflicts were halted for three "days of tranquility" so that some 250,000 children could be vaccinated. Later, in civil wars in Lebanon, Sudan, Uganda, and the former Yugoslavia, warring factions also agreed to a cease-fire for children's health.

Access to safe drinking water was as important as immunization in preventing childhood diseases and in saving children's lives. How does one provide water to rural communities in different geographic regions with contrasting natural environments, using low-cost equipment that does not require specialized skills to operate and maintain? In India's hard-rock areas, the water table was far below the surface and its level was dropping, but in the low land of the Bangladesh delta, flooding occurred regularly. To relieve the water shortage in India, UNICEF developed a deep-well hand pump that was inexpensive and sturdy. The India Mark II water pump has since been used successfully in many other parts of the world. UNICEF used a much simpler technology to provide water in Bangladesh. Shallow tube wells supported by a bamboo scaffold with a simple suction pump on top made a shared hand pump available to every household in a village. To maintain and repair the hand pumps, local volunteers from the community, both men and women, became "village hand pump caretakers." With these "barefoot mechanics," communities took responsibility and ownership for their water supply systems.[21]

Despite significant progress in ensuring child survival, a 1987 UNICEF report, *State of the World's Children*, described the "silent" emergencies killing approximately 280,000 children every week. Frequent infections and undernourishment due to

Because of the efforts of UNICEF and ECHO, a European aid organi-zation, more children and families in developing countries have access to clean water. Clean water is crucial to keeping away diseases caused by unsanitary conditions and unsafe water. The partnership has drilled new wells and built and fixed water systems. Pictured, Carol Bellamy, former head of UNICEF, tries out one of the 12 hand pumps provided by UNICEF in Lodwar, east of Nairobi, Kenya.

poverty and lack of knowledge caused more deaths than any of the "loud" emergencies of famine, droughts, or floods. These silent emergencies were preventable. Over 3 million children a year were dying of dehydration due to diarrhea, which could be prevented by educating families in basic health care and by providing oral rehydration therapy, which costs less than one dollar. Three and a half million children were dying every year of diseases that could be prevented by immunization. The good news was that in the 1980s, the world had "for the first time, the knowledge and the means to defeat infection and undernutrition among the world's children on a massive scale and at an affordable cost." UNICEF therefore could confidently say that with the commitment of governments and societies, "the decade ahead could be one of new hope for the world's children."[22] An important forerunner of new hope was the UN General Assembly's unanimous approval of the Convention on the Rights of the Child.

THE RIGHTS OF THE CHILD COME OF AGE: 1990s

Adopted on November 20, 1989, the Convention on the Rights of the Child gained force as international law on September 2, 1990. During the same month, UNICEF convened the World Summit for Children. At this important moment in UNICEF's history, 159 countries committed to a plan of action with a set of goals for pursuing children's rights and for ensuring their survival, protection, and development. These goals included reducing infant mortality and malnutrition and providing access to health services, education, water, and sanitation.

Although UNICEF and other organizations had brought attention to the issues of children's rights in the past, there was no formal international legal code that demanded recognition and compliance. The Convention lays out in very specific terms the rights of children, and it also establishes the legal duties of governments to ensure these rights. Governments have to report regularly to the Committee on the Rights of the Child on ways in which they take care of children and guarantee their rights.

UNICEF has assumed a significant role as overseer of the Convention's provisions. The social and economic inequities in Latin America are some of the world's worst. Inhabitants still lack basic services and even lack birth certificates. These inequities exclude them from the political and social life of their countries, especially indigenous peoples. In 1998, the government in Peru—one of the most unequal countries in Latin America[23]— with UNICEF, created a program to help poor children obtain birth certificates. They trained 9,000 public registrars and worked with city councils, women's organizations, and soccer clubs to provide free registration for more than 100,000 children lacking official documents. Thousands of these children, previously excluded from education because there were no official records of their births, were then able to attend school.[24] In 1999, UNICEF launched the Meena Communication Initiative and Meena Girl Week in South Asia, as a "mass communication project aimed at changing perceptions and behavior that hamper the survival, protection, and development of girls in South Asia."[25] Using a multimedia package featuring a cartoon character named Meena, messages about gender, child rights, and education are communicated to citizens. The messages discuss the unfair treatment of girls and women and offer positive information from which families and communities can learn.

One of the pillars of children's rights is child protection. As UNICEF embraced the new approach to children's rights, it strengthened its protection efforts. In 1996, UNICEF supported both an international meeting to prevent commercial sexual exploitation of children and a study on the impact of armed conflict on children. UNICEF also started a campaign to ban anti-personnel land mines. Yet, the goal of protection gained more urgency as the twentieth century drew to a close. UNICEF's 2000 *State of the World's Children* report mentioned a "pervasive violence" that ran as a "subtle context" through the lives of women and children.[26] Guided by the priority of children's rights, UNICEF will continue its protection efforts into the next century.

MILLENNIUM DEVELOPMENT GOALS: 2000–

In September 2000, the largest gathering of heads of state and government at that time met in New York for the United Nations Millennium Summit. One hundred and eighty-nine member states of the United Nations agreed on a Millennium Declaration and eight Millennium Development Goals (MDGs) to end global poverty and discrimination by 2015. Six of the eight goals relate directly to children. These goals are:

From September 6–8, 2000, at the largest gathering in history, over 150 world leaders met at the United Nations headquarters in New York. They agreed to help citizens in the world's poorest countries to achieve a better life by 2015. Six of the eight development goals relate directly and are most critical to children.

to eradicate extreme poverty and hunger, to achieve universal primary education, to promote gender equality, to reduce child mortality, to improve maternal health, and to combat HIV/AIDS, malaria, and other diseases. UNICEF plays an important role in achieving these goals for children.

Poverty and hunger describe the daily lives of many children. In Africa, more than 40 percent of people do not have enough food to eat every day. In sub-Saharan Africa, on average 1 out of 6 children dies before age 5.[27] Many women die during pregnancy or childbirth, causing great risk to the baby's life. Diseases like malaria and HIV/AIDS take millions of lives. UNICEF helps to improve the health of children and mothers by supporting and coordinating efforts to educate children, one of the most effective ways to end poverty. UNICEF also works with governments to develop programs that will allow children to survive and thrive.

In developing countries, 1 out of every 10 children is not enrolled in school.[28] In parts of sub-Saharan Africa, North Africa, and the Middle East, one out of every three children has not had any education. Most of these children are girls. Although not by choice, children often are prevented from attending school because they cannot afford to pay the school fees. Some have to work to provide for their families; others are orphans who have to support themselves. In some communities, cultural practices prevent girls from getting an education by forcing them into early marriage or by giving higher priority to the education of boys. Threats of natural disasters and wars disrupt the education of many children even further. Yet education is probably a child's best hedge against poverty. UNICEF helps to fund school supplies, to provide water supplies and sanitation facilities at schools, and to develop a child-friendly curriculum. It also tries to get girls to schools, to encourage them to stay, and to ensure that they have the same opportunities as boys.

Young girls are not only at a disadvantage when it comes to education. A United Nations study in Europe, Africa, and Southeast Asia found that women under the age of 20 have higher rates of infection of HIV than older women or young men. The study states that the genital tracts of young girls are not as developed as those in older women, leaving them prone to sexually transmitted diseases.[29] In an effort to prevent and reduce the risk of HIV infection, UNICEF has made information and services accessible to young women.

UNICEF is the only intergovernmental agency devoted exclusively to children. The world's governments have given UNICEF a mandate to promote and protect children's rights and to ensure their well-being. The MDGs have become part of this mandate. Every action UNICEF takes toward health care, education reform, or child protection is a step toward realizing these goals. UNICEF knows that help for children to reach their full potential is an investment in humanity.

3

Reducing Child Mortality

[W]e could be the first generation to outlaw the kind of extreme, stupid poverty that sees a child die of hunger in a world of plenty, or of a disease preventable by a twenty-cent inoculation. We are the first generation that can afford it. The first generation that can unknot the whole tangle of bad trade, bad debt, and bad luck. The first generation that can end a corrupt relationship between the powerful and the weaker parts of the world which has been so wrong for so long.[30]

—Bono, from foreword to Jeffrey D. Sachs's
The End of Poverty

IS ANY DEATH MORE TRAGIC THAN A CHILD'S DEATH? ALMOST 4 million newborns do not survive their first month. Every

The number of people caught up in emergencies has increased significantly over the years. In addition, the number of ongoing wars has increased and they are lasting longer. One of UNICEF's top objectives is to provide good care, nutrition, and protection to children living under emergency situations like famine, war, and in refugee camps. Above, newly arrived Afghan refugee children carry their belongings through the Jalozai camp in Pakistan.

year, 10 million children die before they reach the age of 5. Even worse, their deaths are preventable by seemingly simple actions. The preventable deaths of children raise child mortality to "public enemy number one" for UNICEF.

UNICEF recognizes that both loud and silent emergencies kill children. Wars, famines, floods, or tsunamis are examples of loud emergencies. Widely publicized on the Internet and on TV, in newspapers and even in films, their devastating and deadly consequences are immediately obvious. More concealed are the silent emergencies of poverty, disease, and hunger in many parts of the world such as Asia, Africa, Latin America, and the Middle East.

Forty years after UNICEF was founded, the 1987 report on the state of the world's children described the "greatest emergency" facing the world's children as the "'silent emergency' of frequent infection and widespread undernutrition." The report continued to describe the impacts of this emergency: "No 'loud emergency,' no famine, no drought, no flood, has ever killed 280,000 children in a week. Yet that is what this silent emergency is now doing—every week."[31] The silent emergency has been more than just a whisper—perhaps it is even a shout or a cry, alerting us that child survival and better health are inseparable.

Child mortality is a health crisis. It is also a food crisis, which affects many parts of the world. Drought, rising food prices, and poverty have left many families without enough food. It also is a global sanitation crisis, which was highlighted when the United Nations declared 2008 as the International Year of Sanitation.

Calling child mortality a crisis indicates its catastrophic proportions. It also acknowledges the difficulties in dealing with this calamity. How does UNICEF respond when confronted with a crisis of this overwhelming nature? Like a skilled problem solver, UNICEF has taken small steps, selecting areas of most importance in which it can have the greatest and most lasting impact. One of its top priorities is child survival. In addition to immunization against infectious diseases, UNICEF has been involved in campaigns to cure diseases and to do away with them where possible. On a smaller scale, UNICEF has provided food to end widespread hunger. UNICEF also has supported rural water supply and sanitation. It is not an exaggeration to say that more people than we can count owe their lives to UNICEF.

THE PROBLEM

Every day thousands of children die of malaria, diarrhea, respiratory infection, AIDS, and other diseases. Many of these children sleep in rooms without anti-malarial bed nets, live in houses without safe drinking water, and die in hospitals without medicines to treat the diseases. Weakened by constant hunger, their bodies offer little or no resistance. Their families and friends are devastated, but to the larger world they die namelessly with no public mention.

The underlying causes of child mortality are related to a lack of resources. Most extremely poor people lack the most basic necessities needed to survive. Not only are they always hungry and lack access to health care, safe drinking water, or sanitation, oftentimes they do not have a home, shelter, or a roof that can keep them dry when it rains. Many children lack basic clothing and shoes. Some of the world's poorest people in countries such as India, Ethiopia, Angola, and Guatemala lack electricity and modern cooking fuels.

On average, people in sub-Saharan Africa have a low life expectancy. There, people can only expect to live until the age of 47, three decades less than the average life expectancy in developed countries.[32] They lack primary care, the basic health care provided by trained health-care workers that is accessible to all and delivered close to where people live and work. It includes health education, prevention, and cures across a variety of diseases and in support of general health. Malaria and HIV/AIDS have claimed the lives of millions of people living in Africa, and these are but two diseases. There are many others hitting that continent with grim force.

Problems of food security in Africa and elsewhere contribute to high death rates. Lack of food security means the absence of regular access to enough food of good quality for healthy and active lives. Countries do not produce enough food to feed their populations. Most of Africa lacks irrigation, and periodic droughts and variable rainfall make it hard for farmers to produce food crops. Soils are generally poor as a result of repeated harvests without adding chemical fertilizers or organic nutrients. Farmers lack fertilizers to grow enough food; they also do not have access to roads to transport food or to markets to distribute food. Hunger is widespread. Yet, Africa is not alone.

MALARIA: A CONTINUING CHALLENGE

According to a 2006 UNICEF report, "Malaria, the number one killer of children in sub-Saharan Africa, remains a formidable enemy."* Scientists discovered over a hundred years ago that malaria is transmitted by a never-ending cycle involving person-mosquito-person. A female bloodsucking *anopheles* mosquito acts as a "vector"—the creature that passes on the microorganisms causing the disease. After feeding on an infected person, the mosquito harbors the parasite, and then deposits it into the bloodstream of another person. Once infected, a person with malaria experiences fevers, or ultimately death.

Neither scientific proofs of the transmission of malaria nor efforts to eradicate it have been able to eliminate this deadly pest. The malaria eradication program with which UNICEF was once associated relied on spraying DDT (dichloro-diphenyl-trichloro-ethane), a poisonous substance that stayed lethal for insects after being sprayed onto surfaces, such as the walls of homes. Despite massive organizational efforts and large sums of money, the eradication program failed. Some of the reasons for the failure involved human behavior; others involved insect behavior. It turned out to be impossible for the anti-malaria sprayers to catch up with the regular migrations of people. Even if they could, mud huts tended to absorb the poison and to reduce its potency. Some mosquitoes

INFECTION AND INFECTIOUS DISEASES

Infectious diseases are prevalent in developing countries where co-infection is common. According to the Global Health Council, between 14 and 17 million people die each year due to infectious diseases—nearly all live in developing countries.[33] Most of these diseases are not necessarily the most

modified their behavior to avoid landing on surfaces covered with DDT, while others became resistant to the poison. Because it proved to be very dangerous to wildlife, DDT ultimately became the target of conservation groups who saw it as a symbol of ways in which human beings were poisoning the earth. Many countries banned its use altogether.

After the failure of the malaria eradication campaign, the emphasis has shifted to the control and treatment of malaria. As new treatments become available, many countries have started to use new drug therapies. Scientists have made some progress in developing a vaccine. While a vaccine is not yet available, UNICEF has worked to increase the coverage of insecticide-treated mosquito nets. The Spread the Net campaign's goal is to provide bed nets to protect people against mosquitoes that carry malaria. Teenagers are already familiar with a variety of nets such as fishing nets, basketball nets, tennis nets, and soccer nets. A mosquito net is different in one major way: it can save the life of an African child. Donating $10 to buy a mosquito net has become a popular way for teenagers around the world to show they care.

---

* UNICEF Annual Report 2006, 12. Available online at *http://www.unicef.org/publications/files/Annual_Report_2006.pdf.*

exotic or the hardest to treat, but the adverse impact among the poorest people is severe because they lack access to needed integrated health care, prevention tools, and treatment. Millions of newborns do not live to see their fifth birthday.

Pneumonia

Pneumonia, which is well known and treatable, is the number one cause of death in children under the age of five; it kills more children than AIDS, malaria, and measles combined. Pneumonia causes the deaths of approximately 2 million children under 5 each year, one fifth of the total number of deaths. The majority of these deaths occur in Africa and in Southeast Asia.[34]

Tuberculosis

Tuberculosis epidemics—where the disease spreads rapidly from one individual to another—have occurred at various times throughout history in developed as well as poor countries. Tuberculosis is a respiratory illness that attacks the lungs. It is especially prevalent among children living in crowded towns, cities, slums, and shantytowns. After World War II, tuberculosis cases—also known as the white plague because those who suffered from the disease were very pale—increased dramatically throughout Europe. In most parts of Europe, around half of all children were infected at the time. Due to poor housing, crowded living conditions, and the lack of sanitation, large numbers of people, especially children, became infected.

Today, tuberculosis continues to threaten children around the world living in impoverished, overcrowded areas without access to clean water or sanitation. Children suffering from tuberculosis have a persistent cough, lose a lot of weight, and are always tired, but these symptoms may only occur long after a child has been infected with the disease. To make matters worse, tuberculosis often accompanies other harmful diseases, such as malaria or diarrhea.

HIV/AIDS

One of the gravest diseases threatening humanity today is HIV/AIDS because of the way it attacks the immune system. Advanced HIV infection often allows other serious infections to invade the lungs, brain, eyes, and other organs. It is very common for persons infected with HIV also to be infected with tuberculosis. Many AIDS patients die of pneumonia.

UNICEF executive director Ann Veneman outlines some dire statistics about the world we live in: "Every minute of every day, a child dies because of AIDS. And every day, there are nearly 1,800 new HIV infections among children under 15." About 2.3 million children are infected with HIV/AIDS, and 15 million are orphaned after their parents die. HIV/AIDS devastates communities and entire countries.[35]

HIV stands for the human immunodeficiency virus, the virus that causes AIDS. HIV infects the white blood cells—an essential part of the body's immune system that defends against infections and disease. Because HIV weakens the immune system, the body cannot protect itself against illness, making it easier for a person to develop deadly diseases. The most advanced stage of HIV infection is known as AIDS, an acronym for acquired immunodeficiency syndrome. *Acquired* means that the illness is not inherited or genetic; *syndrome* refers to a group of symptoms or illnesses that result from the HIV infection. Even before a person with HIV develops any symptoms, called the asymptomatic phase, the person can still infect others.

The most common way in which children are infected with HIV is through transmission from mother to child during pregnancy, labor and delivery, or breastfeeding. HIV also can be passed on through contact with blood, sexual contact, or injection with infected needles.

Ninety percent of all children with HIV/AIDS live in sub-Saharan Africa. For those children, whose life expectancy has plunged from 60 to 30 years, middle age sets in at about age

18. A 17-year-old Nigerian youth describes the horrors of letting the devastating disease go unchecked: "[T]here may be no tomorrow or the world will be full of oldies."[36]

Diarrhea

It is hard to believe, but a simple case of diarrhea also can lead to death. Most cases of diarrhea are caused by some kind of infection. The World Health Organization estimates that nearly 2 million children under the age of five die from diarrhea every year.[37] Most at risk are malnourished children and very young children between six months and three years of age. These children are the most vulnerable because their bodies have a smaller amount of fluid. Diarrhea is so serious because it drains the body of essential fluid, salts, and minerals. When the body is dehydrated, death can occur within hours. In developing nations, each child has an average of four cases a year. Although diarrhea affects millions of children every year, it is particularly prevalent in poor and crowded areas without clean drinking water.

Cholera

Diarrhea and infectious diseases are common where water is dirty, public sanitation is inadequate to remove human and animal waste, and personal hygiene is difficult. The most severe diarrheal disease is cholera, an acute infection of the intestine that can occur where water supplies, sanitation, food safety, and hygiene practices are poor. Cholera causes diarrhea and vomiting, which, if untreated, can lead to rapid dehydration and death. A cholera epidemic gripped politically troubled Zimbabwe in 2008, sending sufferers over the border into South Africa, where they had higher hopes of lifesaving treatment.

For millions of people in developing countries, clean water is not a reality. Because many homes do not have toilets, human waste adds to the impurities in the water supply.

Disposal of human waste is not a topic with mass appeal, so the topic is not often discussed openly. Fortunately, the UN recognized the seriousness of the global sanitation crisis in 2008, when it declared that year the International Year of Sanitation.

FOOD SHORTAGE AND MALNUTRITION

According to the World Health Organization, malnutrition (a medical condition caused by an inadequate or improper diet) is the single gravest threat to the world's health and is associated with about half of all child deaths worldwide.[38] Malnourished children have lowered resistance to infection; they are more likely to die from diarrheal diseases, respiratory infections, malaria, and AIDS. Otherwise simple ailments, if not treated quickly, can become deadly if children also suffer from severe malnutrition. In countries where malnutrition is most devastating—India, Somalia, and Ethiopia—no other condition contributes more to child mortality and illness.

A food crisis is increasing in many parts of the world. In Ethiopia, because of drought, the rising price of food, and low family income, many families do not have enough to eat. Small children suffer acute malnutrition. Underweight, they have emaciated arms and legs that are often no thicker that an adult thumb, in contrast to their bloated bellies. Under stretched skin, their ribs are visible. If the condition continues for a long time, children stop growing and become stunted, meaning that they have low height for their age.

Village health workers or volunteers working for organizations such as Doctors without Borders use a simple diagnostic tool consisting of a color-coded bracelet to measure each child's middle upper-arm circumference. If the bracelet shows green, the child is well nourished. If the bracelet shows yellow, orange, or red, the child may be at risk of malnutrition or may need supplementary feeding or treatment.

Many children in developing countries are hungry. They are forced to survive on less than 1,000 calories per day—less than

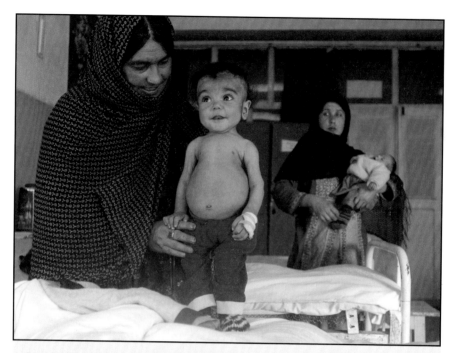

Since its founding, UNICEF has been committed to nutrition programs aimed at fulfilling every child's right to adequate nutrition. UNICEF has worked with religious, government, and community leaders around the world to solicit support for various health programs. Here, a severely malnourished boy at the Indira Ghandi Children's Hospital in Afghanistan gets help standing from his grandmother.

half of what is minimally required to sustain a human being. These children are unlike most children in North America and in Europe, who have enough food to meet their dietary energy requirements—900 calories per day for a 1-year-old to 1,800 calories per day for a 14–18-year-old girl and 2,200 calories per day for a 14–18-year-old boy.[39]

Malnutrition is not only the result of too little food. It is a condition that also results from a lack of essential nutrients. Even when a child is not hungry, she may suffer from poor nutrition because she lacks nutrients such as vitamin A or iodine. Vitamin A, found in liver, eggs, fruit, carrots, and green leafy vegetables, helps prevent infections. Without it, children can develop eye problems and even go blind. Lack of iodine can cause mental retardation. Thus, providing children with more food does not necessarily cure malnutrition; it is important that the food has enough essential nutrients.

UNICEF'S RESPONSE TO THE WORLD'S NEEDS

UNICEF's work in the field of children's public health in all different regions of the world has required close cooperation with other UN agencies, national and local governments, health providers, and communities. In particular, UNICEF has worked closely with the World Health Organization. UNICEF's role has been mainly to assist in providing the necessary supplies such as food, medicines, and health equipment. It also has been very effective in training health workers, raising funds, and creating publicity campaigns to make sure that the world remains aware of children's health and welfare as an essential concern.

One of UNICEF's most significant health victories has been in promoting vaccinations. Major infectious diseases for which there are vaccines available include diphtheria, whooping cough, tetanus, poliomyelitis (polio), measles, and tuberculosis. Immunization always has been an important focus of UNICEF's public health work since its early successes with a mass campaign to vaccinate against tuberculosis in Europe.

The mass immunization campaign in Poland, the largest one that was undertaken in Europe, showed the effectiveness of international teams of both specialists and lay people working together. Sixty Scandinavian doctors and nurses worked together with a number of Polish medical experts and volunteers. This successful immunization campaign significantly lowered the incidences of tuberculosis among children.

The tuberculosis immunization campaign signaled a new period in international public health. Immunization campaigns in Latin America and the Caribbean successfully rid these regions of polio. Measles vaccines given to millions of African children in Angola represent an effort to eliminate this preventable killer of children.

UNICEF has convinced presidents and prime ministers to mobilize whole nations to take part in immunization drives. In 1984 in Colombia, for example, President Belisario Betancur agreed to arrange three days of vaccinations, one month apart. Over 10,000 immunization posts were established in health clinics, schools, community centers, and even in parks and marketplaces. Over 120,000 volunteers helped to arrange the vaccinations and about 13,000 aides were trained to help vaccinate children. In addition, parents were reminded to bring their children for their immunizations on the designated days by teachers, by notes that were included in bank statements, and by priests. President Betancur even immunized a child at the presidential palace in Bogotá. Trained volunteers went by boats to small towns deep in the jungles to visit homes, to inform families of the three national vaccination days, and to make sure they bring their children to be immunized. This successful immunization drive became known as the "showpiece of the international immunization crusade."[40]

UNICEF's immunization campaign in Colombia was so successful that in 1985, El Salvador put a halt to its bloody civil war. Both sides to the conflict agreed to stop fighting for three "days of tranquility." The former executive director of UNICEF, James P. Grant, said of this miraculous event: "Great things are possible—even in a country at war, like El Salvador. For the first time in history, a major conflict has stopped to immunize children."[41] The success of the "days of tranquility" in El Salvador was repeated during civil wars in Uganda, Lebanon, Sudan, and the former Yugoslavia.

Treating Diarrhea

A cure for disease does not have to be costly. That became clear when experiments in Bangladesh during the 1970s proved that dehydration as a result of diarrhea could be treated with a simple oral saline solution that also contained a small quantity of sugar. Medical practitioners saw this very simple and inexpensive remedy as one of the most important medical developments of the century. Yet, it was not widely used to cure dehydration.

UNICEF set out to change this neglect of a cheap and effective remedy that could cure a life-threatening condition. As part of its child survival and development revolution, UNICEF started to provide oral rehydration salts in a pre-mixed packet to which only boiled water had to be added. UNICEF is aware that a little packet of oral rehydration salts would not be able to solve all the factors that cause diarrhea in most poverty-stricken environments—the lack of good food, lack of access to clean water and sanitation, and unhygienic habits. Yet, at least, oral rehydration salts could stall an immediate threat to a child's survival when dehydration already has occurred.

Fighting HIV/AIDS

HIV/AIDS is a complex and devastating disease for which there is no vaccination. Only a concerted worldwide campaign can deal with the enormous problem of AIDS. In an attempt to mobilize efforts to deal with this disastrous disease, UNICEF launched *Unite for Children and Unite Against AIDS*. UNICEF ambitiously aims to reach children at all stages of life, from infants to adolescents.

The main way to protect infants from infection by HIV is to prevent the spread of the disease from mother to child. In order to accomplish this goal, pregnant women are encouraged to get tested. If a pregnant woman tests positive for HIV, treatment can be provided to protect the woman's own health and to reduce the chances that her baby will be born with the disease. Also the mother receives counseling on the best feeding options for the baby.

The behavior of some adolescents puts them at special risk that they will acquire HIV. Risky behavior includes unprotected

After UNICEF urged Asian countries to beef up HIV education and pre-vention programs, Malaysian officials signed a deal with UNICEF to open a research center at the Health Management Institute in Kuala Lumpur, Malaysia. In 2005, UNICEF launched the Unite for Children Unite against AIDS campaign, and Malaysia was the twenty-fourth country to take part. Above, UNICEF workers in Kuala Lumpur distribute *Children and HIV/AIDS* booklets.

sex with an infected partner or using dirty needles when tak-ing drugs. Young people who receive accurate information and education in life skills are less likely to engage in these risky behaviors. Skills that are especially helpful include the ability to make informed decisions, to solve problems, to think criti-cally, to cope with stress, and to negotiate difficult situations. With good information and the necessary life skills, young people may adjust their behavior to reduce their risk through abstinence, faithfulness, condom use, and substance-abuse treatment. UNICEF and others have supported the distribution of information through mass media and person-to-person, as well as peer education. Important services for youth include drug and sex counseling, HIV-testing, and treating sexually transmitted infections.

Young women face special risks of becoming infected with HIV. Rape and sexual abuse of young women and children are major causes of new HIV infections in South Africa. In 1999, UNICEF and England's Manchester United football (soccer) team began a nine-year partnership to create programs to tackle violence through education. In lively workshops, athletes and South African youth explored the attitudes and behaviors that can lead to HIV transmission. The partnership has raised substantial funds to help children worldwide who are suffering from AIDS. Equally important, it has encouraged greater respect for women and healthier behavior. In 2008, the partnership was extended to 2010. This will be the longest standing public-private partnership between a premier football club and an international charity.

Because of the complex and devastating nature of AIDS, prevention is very important, but so is caring for adults and children who already have HIV/AIDS. UNICEF and others are working to increase access to treatment in developing countries where its citizens cannot afford the expensive drugs which help to extend and improve the quality of life. In Lesotho, in southern Africa, UNICEF sponsors a clinic that provides real hope to infected children. After seven-year-old Kananelo received the diagnosis that he had HIV, the clinic provided him with antiretroviral (ARV) treatment. Before he started treatment, his immune system was failing and he had an infection in his lungs. Kananelo could not afford to buy the expensive drugs that would inhibit the replication of the virus. Fortunately Kananelo did not become another tragic statistic. Due to effective treatment, he is growing, gaining weight, and is back in school; he seems pretty much like any healthy child.[42]

UNICEF also supports children who live with sick or dying parents, or who have lost one or both parents to AIDS. Such children face health risks; they often have to stop going to school; they lack clothing and food; they feel depressed and anxious. They may even be abused in their communities because nobody protects them. UNICEF has helped very poor families in countries such as Malawi and Kenya to buy food, to allow children to go back to school, and to gain a sense of dignity.

Treating Malnutrition

UNICEF has raised millions of dollars to respond to the nutrition, health, education, water, sanitation, and hygiene needs of children in drought-affected areas of countries like Ethiopia and Somalia. It has trained health workers to treat severe malnutrition. The condition of a small child with swollen hands, feet, and face can improve in just three to six weeks after the child is given specially treated milk and high protein biscuits called plumpy nut. Another way to treat malnutrition is with a nutritionally dense spread consisting of about 500 calories. This ready-to-use food comes in a packet containing milk powder and essential nutrients. Such ready-to-use foods have several advantages: they do not need any preparation, they have a long shelf life, they are easy to transport, and they are easy to use in hot climates.

UNICEF provides essential nutrients in other forms. In health centers, UNICEF workers regularly provide vitamin A to children when they vaccinate or examine them. More universally, to prevent mental retardation, UNICEF has promoted the addition of low-cost iodine to table salt.

Providing Access to Clean Water and Sanitation

UNICEF works in nearly 100 countries to improve water supplies, to build sanitation facilities in schools and communities, and to promote safe hygiene practices and cleanliness.

UNICEF country programs support activities such as drilling wells and erecting hand pumps.

THE FUTURE

In 1990, 93 children of every 1,000 died before age 5. By 2015, the UN hopes to fulfill one of its Millennium Development Goals by decreasing this number to 31 of every 1,000.

Because children are central to the achievement of these goals, UNICEF has an important role in making the development goals of this millennium a reality.

Yet UNICEF is limited in what it can do to ease this crisis. Mass deaths of children occur day after day. Children die because of hunger and diseases, many of which are treatable and preventable. Lives are wasted due to extreme poverty and lack of development. Cutting poverty will only be possible if the world's richest countries move beyond promises of giving more help to developing nations. Moreover, individuals also need to do their share. Every woman, man, girl, and boy can play a small part in improving the lot of others, in doing away with misery, and in creating hope.

Basic Education
for All

Study after study has taught us that there is no tool for development more effective than the education of girls. No other policy is as likely to raise economic productivity, lower infant and maternal mortality, improve nutrition and promote health—including helping to prevent the spread of HIV/AIDS. No other policy is as powerful in increasing the chances of education for the next generation.[43]

—Kofi A. Annan, Secretary-General of the
United Nations, foreword to "The State
of the World's Children 2004: Girls,
Education and Development"

LEARNING IS IMPORTANT FOR THE PERSONAL DEVELOPMENT and well-being of every girl or boy. It can provide girls and boys with knowledge and skills necessary to lead healthier lives and to protect themselves against HIV/AIDS and other diseases. For poor families, education can be a way out of poverty. As children make the transition to adolescence and adulthood, education can prepare them to take an active role in making social, economic, and political decisions. Advancement in education benefits societies in many ways. It leads to better citizenship, better economic development, and better services.

UNICEF has focused on providing all children, especially those who are most excluded and most vulnerable, with a basic education, and on ensuring equal education for both boys and girls. In a coordinated, joint effort by the United Nations Educational, Scientific and Cultural Organization (UNESCO); the United Nations Development Program (UNDP); UNICEF; the United Nations Population Fund (UNFPA); and the World Bank, the Education for All Global Action Plan aims to meet the learning needs of all children, youth, and adults by 2015.

PROBLEM: ACCESS TO BASIC, QUALITY EDUCATION

Societies, unequal in wealth and opportunities, exclude millions of children, especially girls, from school. UNICEF estimates that 93 million children are out of school, including children who are enrolled but do not attend classes. Almost 80 percent of children who are not in school live in sub-Saharan Africa and South Asia—in countries such as India, Pakistan, and Bangladesh.[44] Across the globe, children who grow up in poverty, who face ethnic discrimination, and who have suffered from natural disasters and other emergencies are likely to miss out on opportunities for education. More than half of the children who are absent from school are girls.

Many children do not receive a basic education. For example, Lalita Kumari grew up in Bihar, India, as a member of a

To achieve their goal of quality basic education for all children, UNICEF has developed programs focused on those most vulnerable: girls, the disabled, ethnic minorities, the rural and urban poor, victims of war and natural disasters, and children affected by HIV/AIDS. Above, students in West Bengal, India, study on the floor of their dilapidated primary school.

caste traditionally looked down upon as "unclean" because they perform menial or "dirty" tasks such as cleaning bathrooms, working leather, or slaughtering animals. As a young girl, she spent her days "doing nothing but cutting grass, fetching fire-wood, cleaning and cooking."[45] In her community, many other girls her age have never attended or have not completed primary school. Not having learned basic literacy and math, they do not have the option to continue to the secondary level. The female literacy rate is among the lowest in the country, about one in three women are unable to read. Girls like Lalita face terrible disadvantages.

UNICEF'S RESPONSE

Access to education opens the doors to learning literacy, numeracy (proficiency in math), and other basic skills. These doors have been opened for Lalita Kumari. In her region of Bihar, India, disadvantaged girls aged 9 to 15 who have never attended or completed primary school are now able to attend a day school, called an Awakening Center, to learn basic literacy and numeracy. After starting at this center, Lalita was asked if she would like to attend an eight-month course at the Mahila Shiksan Kendra, an education center for adolescent girls who are semi-literate. Lalita was thrilled at the opportunity for learning, but her father believed that girls should stay home. It took some convincing before her father allowed her to attend. At the Mahila Shiksan Kendra, Lalita received not only a basic education, but also training in life skills, analytical skills to help her in personal and social situations, leadership skills, and even karate as part of a curriculum that aims to develop the whole person. Lalita successfully graduated after reaching grade 5. With a more positive self-image, she has set her goal on continuing her education up to grade 10. While working toward this goal, she finds joy in teaching karate to younger girls who say, "[we] want to be strong like [her]."[46]

PROBLEM: ACCESS TO AFFORDABLE EDUCATION

While most countries' enrollment rates in primary schools are above 80 percent, in South Asia the rates are as low as 74 percent, and sub-Saharan Africa lags behind that at a shocking 59 percent.[47] A pressing issue for many poor families is that they cannot afford tuition. Even if there are no tuition fees, textbooks, uniforms, and examinations can be costly. Ten-year-old Silvia Akinyi lives in Kibera, one of the poorest areas in Nairobi, where the average family income is about $27 a month. Her father, who works at small jobs, was not able to raise $133 to enroll her in school. In his mind, "school [is] for the rich and not for poor people like us."[48]

UNICEF'S RESPONSE

For those who cannot afford school fees, free education is essential. Experience has shown that the removal of school fees leads to a significant increase in enrollment. In Kenya, during the first year after the government adopted a free primary education policy, more than 1.3 million children entered school for the first time.[49] The increase in numbers created new challenges. As some classrooms doubled in size, they had too few desks and not enough stationery and equipment. In 2002, UNICEF and the Kenyan government jointly started the child-friendly primary school initiative with the goals of improving school quality and making it possible for children to at least complete primary school. UNICEF provided textbooks, desks, and chalk. It also supported the training of thousands of teachers to enable them to turn classrooms into stimulating learning environments.

PROBLEM: LACK OF SANITARY SCHOOLS, SEPARATE TOILETS, AND CLEAN WATER

Education for girls can be hindered by the absence of something as basic as a girls-only restroom. Hassina Mohammed, a 12-year-old girl in the fourth grade at Gewane Primary School in Ethiopia's Afar region, explains why girls are uncomfortable when all students have to share bathrooms: "Boys are messy and don't keep the toilets clean, which makes it uncomfortable for us girls. When we tell them to clean up they tease and make fun of us."[50] Especially when girls reach puberty, they are embarrassed to share toilets with boys.

UNICEF'S RESPONSE

It may seem simple, but the provision of separate bathrooms for boys and girls can be a very important component of strategies for increasing girls' enrollment in school and creating a favorable learning environment. This is true of many sanitation measures. In the Afar region of Ethiopia, where the temperature can climb to 104°F during the cool season and only 31 percent of households have access to safe water, UNICEF has launched a water and sanitation project. As part of this project, a new toilet block was built for the Gewane Primary School, which has made girls like Hassina Mohammed feel much more comfortable. Outside the toilet block are newly constructed taps. A UNICEF poster with a photograph of an Afar girl washing her hands reads in bold lettering: "Your health is in your hands. Always wash them."[51]

PROBLEM: UNEQUAL TREATMENT IN SCHOOLS

Even where girls are able to attend school, many schools do not provide equal education to boys and girls. A study in Zambia found that teachers appreciate and encourage boys' participation in class more than girls' contributions. To make matters worse, school tasks such as sweeping floors and cleaning toilets are reserved for girls. And the learning environment often does not protect children against violence and abuse. When girls experience sexual, physical, or emotional violence, their access to education and their ability to learn are impeded. When violence occurs at school, silence often surrounds the issue, making diagnosis and prevention difficult.

Gender equality is not just about girls. Although girls are often left out of schools, boys also have certain disadvantages. In some countries boys are underperformers or they completely disappear from the school system. In countries in Latin America and the Caribbean, boys are more likely than girls to be absent and to repeat grades. In Brazil, at around the age of

 RWANDA AFTER THE GENOCIDE

Not all disasters are natural. Some of the world's great disasters are generated by people. The effects of these emergencies can last even longer than those of natural disasters. Children in Rwanda live with memories of family members being killed during the 1994 conflict, when Hutu systematically killed an estimated 800,000 Tutsi in an attempt to destroy the whole ethnic group. A UNICEF study found that 96 percent of Rwandan children had witnessed the mass murders and 80 percent had lost at least one family member. As a result of the killings, along with the epidemic of HIV/AIDS, hundreds of thousands of Rwandan children were orphaned.[*]

As a consequence, fewer than half of Rwandan girls complete primary school. One reason for the high dropout rates among girls is that girls help to support their families. Many older girls have to fulfill the role of a parent in one of the thousands of child-headed households. Still, in Rwanda it is not only poverty and the demands of work that keep girls out of school. Sexual harassment and violence against girls are common obstacles to girls' schooling. So is the mistaken belief that girls cannot succeed, especially in science.

While Rwanda is still recovering from the 1994 bloodbath, the spread of HIV has made the healing process more difficult. To help children experience childhood amid memories of war and the current epidemic, UNICEF has helped to establish child-friendly schools. Focusing on the "whole" child, these schools not only pro-

10, boys begin to leave school at a higher rate than girls. Men in Brazil have on average fewer years of formal education: 5.7 years as compared to 6.0 years for women.[52] When Anderson was a boy in his early teens in Rio de Janeiro, Brazil, he thought it was cool to hang out with his male friends or to play soccer on the street instead of sitting in a classroom. He remembers,

vide girls and boys with a positive teaching and learning environment, but they also offer counseling and mentoring.

Since fewer than half of Rwandan girls graduate from primary school, teachers and others reach out to the community to try to convince parents of the benefits of education, even if the family is on a tight budget. Mukarimba followed a typical pattern for girls by dropping out of school to work on the family farm. After Mukarimba left school, teachers went to her house to talk to her mother, who finally allowed Mukarimba to return to school.[**]

Gender equality is an important part of education at child-friendly schools in Rwanda. Key features of every school are the *Tuseme* clubs—named after the Swahili word for "Let's speak out"—where girls and boys are encouraged to speak their minds. As a result of a Tuseme club, girls and boys realize they can perform many of the same tasks. A boy at a Tuseme club remarked: "Before, the girls swept the classroom alone. Now, we all sweep together."[***]

---

[*] Sarah Crowe, "Helping Orphans in Rwanda Build a Better Future," UNICEF. Available online at *http://www.unicef.org/infobycountry/rwanda_31013.html.*

[**] Stephanie Wang-Breal, "Child-friendly Schools Help Young Rwandans Rediscover Childhood," UNICEF. Available online at *http://www.unicef.org/infobycountry/rwanda_44730.html.*

[***] Ibid.

"My mother would call me to go to school and I would say that I wasn't going. And I'd take off running because there was no man at the house . . . a man who could run after me and catch me and make me go to school."[53] It is increasingly widespread, even in developed countries, for adolescent boys to drop out of school and to shun academic work.

UNICEF'S RESPONSE

UNICEF supports recruiting and training teachers who are sensitive to gender rights and who understand that in Zambia, like in other countries, girls as well as boys should be encouraged to participate and to feel valued for their contributions. Recruiting and training more female teachers to serve as role models for girls can help to create an environment that is sensitive to the needs of both boys and girls. When girls are given a chance, they can inspire changes in the character of the school system and spur communities to work toward providing quality and equal education for all. In 2001, girls' potential across Africa was recognized with the launching of the Girls' Education Movement. Girls participating in this organization identify children who are out of school and take the initiative to bring them to school. As a result, girls' enrollment has increased. More importantly, the program has demonstrated that girls can be active and vocal participants in education. The movement also encourages boys to participate as active advocates of gender-sensitive education.

What about boys' education? Although boys can be strategic allies to promote girls' rights, there is no simple solution to the problem of boys' underachievement and disaffection with education. There are programs that try to empower boys and to extend their education. The Youth Empowerment and Skills Training program in the Bahamas works with young men who have trouble with the regular school curriculum. The Uplifting Adolescents Project in Jamaica concentrates on adolescents who are not in school and who are unemployed. Many of the

Although girls have unequal access to education, boys also must over-come disadvantages. Boys are more likely than girls to drop out of school or to avoid academic work. Still, schools like this one in Iraq have become a refuge for children affected by displacement, poverty, and conflict. In December 2008, UNICEF and the Nokia Corporation announced a part-nership to rebuild eight primary schools in two of the poorest areas in southern Iraq and the northern Kurdish region.

young men in these programs come from families with low incomes and low social status. Their socialization in the home plays an important part in how they view education and learn-ing. They experience similar problems to Anderson in Brazil whom we read about earlier, partly because he had no father who was involved with his development and who supported his education. Without the example or assistance of a father, Anderson had to learn the hard way that education could ben-efit him more than the call of the streets. In his late teens, after experiencing how hard it was to survive without an education, Anderson decided to go back to school. He explained, "I'm gonna study. Without an education . . . it's already hard."[54] The challenge remains to find ways to counter some boys' negative experiences and to create schools that are sensitive to the needs of both boys and girls.

PROBLEM: FAILURE TO TEACH BASIC LIFE SKILLS

Education is of poor quality when it ignores the social factors that impede learning or attendance. It is also inferior if it fails to provide the life skills that make it possible to lead a productive life. A big question for many countries is: What does it take to thrive in a world with HIV and AIDS, conflict, violence, and gender and ethnic discrimination? Students are often ignorant when it comes to basic life skills. In Turkmenistan there is very little knowledge about ways to prevent AIDS. Less than one in eight women are able to identify how HIV is passed on.

UNICEF'S RESPONSE

Through the United Nations Girls' Education Initiative (UNGEI), UNICEF is promoting life-skills-based education with a gender focus. Education focusing on life skills accepts that females face risks to their health and safety that make it harder to learn. Risks include alcohol consumption, tobacco and drug use, malnutrition, and disease. To avoid these risks, girls and women need more than just information; they also need skills to make the right decisions and to negotiate difficult situations.

Girls who participated in a life-skills training program at School Number 45 in Yoloten Etrap, in eastern Turkmenistan, have shed much of their ignorance about HIV/AIDS. As Aybegench Tugunova, 15, explains, "Many of us used to think that HIV could be passed on even by somebody just breathing on you. Now we know exactly how the virus is transmitted and how we can protect ourselves."[55] Through life-skills training, the pupils now know that HIV can be passed on in four general ways: through sexual intercourse; by sharing contaminated needles for drug use; through blood transfusion; and by mother-child transmission during pregnancy, childbirth, and breastfeeding.

PROBLEM: MISTREATMENT BY TEACHERS

A quality, basic education depends on many interrelated factors, which can be summed up in a single requirement: schools have to be "child-friendly." In 2004, when children from 51 districts in Pakistan were invited to send a message to the president of the country urging him to provide a quality education to every child, many of the 32,000 postcards that the president received focused on the need to create a child-friendly learning environment. Factors that make the environment in Pakistan unfriendly to children include the frequent use of corporal punishment in schools and at home, and the ridiculing of children by teachers and other adults. Children often feel maltreated, not understood, and not respected.

UNICEF'S RESPONSE

UNICEF promotes child-friendly schools that focus on the "whole" child—including health, nutrition, and overall well-being. They aim to make education a positive experience for all children. Child-friendly schools combine opportunities for learning in a safe and healthy environment with community involvement. They address both the substance and the process of learning. What is the substance of learning? Mastering a core academic curriculum is not enough. It is just as important for children to learn life skills and to develop self-esteem and self-confidence as it is for them to learn to read, write, and count. How do children learn best? Clearly, not by being preached at but by being involved in active and participatory learning. The learning environment has to be unprejudiced, unbiased, and sensitive to the needs of both boys and girls. The learning

environment has to be safe, which means no corporal punishment and no physical, sexual, or mental harassment. The
learning environment has to be healthy, which requires safe
water, adequate sanitation, and separate toilet facilities for girls
and boys. To create a positive learning environment for all, a
child-friendly school depends on the involvement of children,
families, and communities, with particular sensitivity to the
needs of vulnerable children.

THE FUTURE OF EDUCATING ALL CHILDREN

Quality education remains a distant dream for many children.
Nonetheless, at the Millennium Summit in 2000, world leaders committed themselves to achieving universal primary
education and to eliminating gender disparities at all levels
of education by 2015. To reach the goal of universal primary
education, countries must first enroll all school-age children, and then keep them in school. According to a World
Bank study, only 34 developing countries (32 percent) have
achieved universal primary education, and another 28 countries are likely to achieve that goal (26 percent). The remaining 42 percent of countries are at risk of not achieving the goal
unless they make faster progress. The goal of gender parity
similarly remains elusive: For every 100 boys out of school,
there are 117 girls in the same situation.[56]

UNICEF recognizes that, "[f]or the Education Goal to
be met, actions need to address both human and material
needs—buildings, books, and teachers—and the organic
requirements of getting all children into school and ensuring they complete a quality education. These include gender
equality in society, good health and nutrition, and the strong
backing of governments and communities."[57] As a result,
UNICEF participated in global information campaigns to
raise awareness about the importance of getting children
to school, especially girls. One such campaign, "Go Girls!
Education for Every Child," has mobilized resources and pub-

lic support for getting more girls to school in 25 countries. UNICEF has worked with governments to take bold steps, such as abolishing school fees. UNICEF also works directly with communities and families to strengthen their ability to protect and care for children such as those orphaned by AIDS. And for countries that have experienced emergencies, UNICEF provides tents, supplies, and other assistance for mass back-to-school campaigns.

UNICEF recognizes that present efforts are not enough to ensure that every child will complete a full course of primary school by 2015. In partnership with many other organizations, it is always thinking of new strategies that will enable countries to make "quantum leaps" in their enrollment rates and to meet the gender parity goal.

UNICEF'S work with Rwanda has seen great results. Because Rwanda's constitution requires that 30 percent of lawmakers are female, the country has the highest proportion of woman legislators in the world. The Rwandan government realizes that if it is going to continue to have women in leadership positions, it needs to educate girls from a young age. UNICEF works with the government to encourage girls to stay in school and to demonstrate the truth of the old Rwandan proverb, *Umukobwa ni nyampinga*: "A girl is a palace of wealth."[58]

5

Protecting Children from Violence and Abuse

The central message of the [United Nations study on violence against children] is that no violence against children can be justified; all violence against children can and must be prevented. Every society, no matter its cultural, economic, or social background, can and must stop every form of violence.[59]

—Study presented by independent expert
Paulo Sérgio Pinheiro to the Third
Committee of the General Assembly
in New York on October 11, 2006

CHILDREN HAVE A RIGHT TO BE PROTECTED FROM VIOLENT behavior, mistreatment, abuse, and neglect. Sadly, they are often unprotected. Boys and girls risk death, poor physical and mental

An estimated 20 million children have been forced to flee their homes due to conflicts. More than 2 million children have been killed and more than 1 million have been orphaned or separated from their families by armed conflict over the last decade. UNICEF draws attention to the duties of governments, families, communities, and individuals to ensure that all children are protected from violence. This Palestinian boy carries his belongings as a bulldozer demolishes a house next to the border with Egypt, in the Rafah refugee camp on the southern Gaza Strip.

health, disease, educational problems, homelessness, and a life of misery that may later be passed on to their own children.

UNICEF's child protection programs aim to prevent violence, all forms of behavior that take advantage of children, and all forms of ill treatment. The programs also attempt to help children who have suffered abuse, giving special consideration to children who are vulnerable, such as those without parents and those affected by war.

Approximately 218 million children work as child laborers, often doing dangerous work. About 143 million children lack parental care because they have lost one or both parents. As many as 70 million women and girls have experienced a form of female genital mutilation or a cutting away of part or all of their external genitalia. Two million girls are sexually exploited, and in developing countries, more than 60 million women are married before they are 18. About 40 million boys and girls below the age of 15 experience violence or neglect. The births of 51 million babies in developing countries are never registered.[60] Confronting these overwhelming facts, UNICEF strives to promote a protective environment that can respond to and help prevent abuse.

THE MANY FORMS OF VIOLENCE

Violence against children takes many forms. It may consist of physical abuse, such as beating, hitting, kicking, hair pulling, and sexual abuse. Or it may involve mental abuse, such as threats—with or without a weapon—and intimidation. A comment such as "you never do anything right" may not involve physical injury, but it may still be abuse, as it can make a child feel worthless. Violence may also be a form of neglect—for example, when a parent leaves a child alone for a long time, does not feed a child, or does not speak to a child.

Societies often accept forms of violence, such as female genital mutilation or cutting, corporal punishment as a form of discipline, and child marriage. Violence occurs in homes, schools, orphanages, work places, and on the streets. Abusive behaviors are often concealed, and those who commit violent acts often go unpunished. Yet violence against children can seriously hamper their development. It can destroy children's self-confidence, health, and willingness to learn or go to school. Children who experience violence are more likely to be depressed or to commit suicide as adults.

PROBLEM: SEXUAL ABUSE AND EXPLOITATION

The sexual abuse of children is a particularly shocking form of violence, especially when children suffer abuse from an adult who is close to them. Eight-year-old Melati[61] lives with her family on Lombok, one of the thousands of scenic islands that make up the Indonesian archipelago. When her mother noticed one day that she was walking in a strange way, she brought Melati to see a doctor. The doctor found that she had been sexually abused. Melati's alleged rapist was a relative who was also a teacher.

UNICEF'S RESPONSE

Sexual violence against children is almost always concealed from sight. Early recognition is important to prevent and pro-tect children from this kind of traumatic abuse. After Melati had been abused, she and her family sought help from a child protection agency in Indonesia. Supported by UNICEF, this agency made sure that the abuser was tried and that the victim received the necessary support. Support for a girl like Melati involves the help of female police officers who are trained to deal sensitively with other women. Through appropriate and confidential medical care and counseling, Melati and others who experience violence can learn that they need not feel ashamed or guilty, but that it helps to express themselves about violence in their lives.

UNICEF believes that education and open discussion about abuse are critical to protecting children. In Indonesia, children in elementary school learn about their rights, create anti-violence posters, and have lively discussions about the issue. Children are given the tools to protect themselves, including advice on how to avoid dangerous situations. They learn that sometimes the best response when someone tries to harm them is to run, to get away. It is also all right to yell, shout, and call for help when they are in trouble. Also, it is important to tell a trusted friend, teacher, parent, or other grown-up if they are being abused or bullied. If they feel that they cannot talk about what happened, it may be easier to write a note to someone to explain how they feel.

PROBLEM: CHILD LABOR

Child labor is another form of child abuse often hidden from view—by the walls of homes, by the enclosures around work-shops and factories, by the foliage surrounding plantations. One in six children in the world, and one in three children in sub-Saharan Africa, work as child laborers.[62] Not all work that children perform is viewed as child labor. For example, children may work at home, on a family farm, or in a family business, performing work that is not dangerous to their health, does not prevent them from going to school, and still allows them time to play. Child labor only refers to work that damages children's health, threatens their education, and leads to further ill treatment.

Poverty often forces children to seek work when their families can no longer afford to feed them. Shukur, 8, lives near Lake Awassa in Ethiopia. Population increase, severe drought, and rising food prices have made it harder for families to survive. When his family did not have enough to eat, Shukur's mother sent him away from home to find work. He now sleeps with other children on a hard floor and goes out to look for work every morning in Lake Awassa's fishing industry. He often works for four hours, from eight until noon. From the money he earns, he pays a quarter for a place to sleep and a dollar for food. He also tries to save enough to buy a bicycle, "which I will then rent out for 25 cents a ride to the other boys."[63] His hope is that he will earn enough money to go back to school to become a doctor. He cannot know it as he makes these clever but risky plans, but UNICEF will make it possible for Shukur to go back to school without first having to save enough money to buy a bicycle.

UNICEF'S RESPONSE

Child labor is likely to be reduced or eliminated when governments provide every child with access to education. Still, even access to education is not enough to solve the problem. Governments and agencies must know the reasons why children work. Where children are forced into child labor to support families in need, families need help finding alternative income to replace the income from a child's employment. If the parents' attitudes and behavior are to change, they also need to be made aware of the ways in which labor is harmful to a child's health and development. At the same time, parents and communities need to understand the ways in which education can benefit a child.

UNICEF started a project in Ethiopia to ensure education for child laborers in Lake Awassa's fishing industry. Children like Shukur, who were forced to leave home because of their families' difficult circumstances, can now attend an informal school to continue their studies. Children receive clothes and supplies, and they also have access to counseling from a social worker. Under the project, families in the surrounding area also get assistance. To enable parents to generate more income, they have opportunities for job training. Small loans and cash grants are available for individuals who are interested in setting up small businesses. The project helps families to avoid the desperate situation in which they are forced to send their children away.

PROBLEM: EXPLOITATION OF ORPHANS AND OTHER CHILDREN WITHOUT CAREGIVERS

Parents—usually the first line of protection for children—are absent in the lives of many children. For many reasons, millions of children live without the care of their parents. While orphans have lost one or both parents, other children are involuntarily separated from their parents. Street children, for example, often have no contact with caregivers. Similarly, children who are placed in institutions because of disabilities or poverty often lose contact with parents. Separation from

LIFE AFTER BEING A CHILD SOLDIER

"I know the nature of what it is to be forgotten, what it is to lose your humanity, and more importantly, what it is to recover from it and to have another life."* These were the words of Ishmael Beah, UNICEF's first Advocate for Children Affected by War. Ishmael Beah was forcibly recruited as a child soldier in Sierra Leone when he was 13. By the time UNICEF found him, he had lost all hope. He sees his role as a UNICEF advocate to speak for "children who do not have the voice to speak....We're trying to give them that voice. And through my capacity I hope we can bring that voice alive."

Not all child soldiers or former child soldiers are as well known as Ishmael Beah, who wrote the best-selling book *A Long Way Gone: Memoirs of a Boy Soldier.* Around 300,000 children across the world are currently involved in armed conflict. They are forced to use weapons or to perform sexual services for adult fighters. They serve as porters, cooks, domestic servants, or messengers. They experience the horrors of war, and they see friends die in the fighting.

In the Democratic Republic of the Congo (DRC), conflict among different Congolese groups has claimed many lives. The Mayi-Mayi militia, a band of Congolese soldiers, formed a families also occurs when children are kidnapped and held to perform services against their will, such as fighting in wars. A prolonged hospital stay for illness or a period of detention when a child is suspected or convicted of an offense can result in estrangement from one's parents.

Children without the guidance and protection of caregivers are at risk of being abused, exploited, and even killed. If they survive, they often go without food, health care, education, and parental support, all things that promote social and emotional development. Girls, especially, face a serious risk

decade ago in opposition to another group of Congolese, the Rassemblement Congolais pour la Démocratie (RCD), which has the support of Rwanda. About half of the soldiers in the Mayi-Mayi militia are children. Most of them are forced to join the group or are lured into the group by false promises. They are promised that, if they join, bullets aimed at them would magically turn into water. Like *mayi*, the Swahili word for "water," they will become imperishable or everlasting, and they will be able to protect their families and communities from attackers. So they are told.

Willing to die for his country, Maisha (not his real name) joined the militia. He managed to escape a year later, but only after he saw many friends killed and his village burned. Following his escape he joined the Centre pour Transit et Orientation (CTO), a reintegration center for former combatants who were children. At the center, Maisha learned carpentry, mechanics, and masonry. He then started to work as an intern at a thriving carpentry firm.

Many children who manage to leave the armed forces find it much harder to rejoin their communities or to find decent work,

(continues)

(continued)

partly because they lack education, and they suffer from serious psychological or physical damage. Masika (not her real name) decided to join the Rassemblement Congolais pour la Démocratie (RCD) at age 13, after her mother died, in part because she liked the uniforms. She fled five years later because it no longer made sense to her that she was fighting against her own people. "Can you imagine what it's like . . . fighting with people whose blood was the same as yours?" she asked.** She ended up in the same UNICEF-sponsored reintegration center as Maisha. After she spent six months learning to read, write, and sew, she contacted her family, hoping that she could return. But her father, ashamed of her service as a soldier and afraid of possible danger to the family, advised that she live far away.

It is not unusual for girls who return from combat to be outcasts, stigmatized by their families and communities. Madeleine, 15, another former girl soldier who was forcibly recruited by the Mayi-Mayi, asked herself, "What is [the girl soldiers'] future after being demobilized?"*** Now working as an adviser for the reintegration of girl combatants, Madeleine urged the world to recognize the crimes committed against girls who are former fighters and to "ask for forgiveness for these girl soldiers."

---

* Chris Niles, "On CRC Anniversary, Ishmael Beah Appointed UNICEF Advocate for Children Affected by War," UNICEF. Available online at *http://www.unicef.org/protection/index_41894.html.*

** Bent Jorgen Perlmutt, "Masika's Story: Child Combatant in DR Congo Recalls the Emptiness of Army Life," UNICEF. Available online at *http://www.unicef.org/protection/drcongo_41183.html.*

*** Rachel Bonham Carter, "A Former Child Soldier Speaks Out at UN Session on Challenges Facing Girls," UNICEF. Available online at *http://www.unicef.org/protection/index_38532.html.*

of sexual exploitation. Rehan, whose home is the streets of Lahore, Pakistan, is an intelligent, funny teenager with roughly trimmed hair, who dresses in dirty trousers and a tunic with a man's wool jacket, several sizes too big. Rehan, who may be "nearly 18," does not have the typical body type of a teenage boy. That is because Rehan is actually Rehana, a girl who disguised herself as a boy to appear stronger and to avoid many of the dangers to street girls in Lahore. "Can you imagine what would happen to me if I dressed as a girl?" she asks.[64] Rehan(a) received some help from UNICEF.

UNICEF'S RESPONSE

UNICEF works to assist orphans, children who have lost contact with their families, and children who are separated from their parents. UNICEF provides support to families, it supports foster care systems, and it looks for alternatives to large impersonal institutions where children are often unsupervised, where loving care is missing, and where discipline can be too harsh. UNICEF also works with governments to make them aware of crisis situations involving orphans and other vulnerable children and to secure their commitment to fund services and care centers for children without parental care. In Lahore, Pakistan, UNICEF has supported both Nai Zindagi, a drop-in center to help drug addicts with recovery, and Project Smile, a safe haven for street children. After Project Smile's outreach program found Rehana, the girl who disguised herself as a boy to survive on the streets, she can now get help with recovery from drug addiction. Project Smile also provides children with food, clean clothes, health care, counseling, and informal education.

PROBLEM: FEMALE GENITAL MUTILATION

In some cultures, parents and family members subject girls to female genital mutilation or cutting of the external genitalia. The belief is that girls need to have the procedure to be considered suitable for marriage. The procedure is extremely painful and can lead to bleeding and infection. It can cause serious complications during and after childbirth, such as excessive bleeding by the mother and the baby's death. It also can cause lasting shock and psychological suffering.

Practitioners who perform female genital mutilation usually are traditional birth attendants or trained midwives. They get paid well for their services, and they enjoy a certain status in their communities. Haissa,[65] a 45-year-old woman from Niamey, Niger, underwent female genital mutilation when she was 7, and at age 10 she learned to perform the procedure from family members. She performed female genital mutilation on approximately 400 girls, some of whom died after undergoing the procedure.

UNICEF'S RESPONSE

UNICEF works to create awareness of the risks of female genital mutilation. It encourages governments to pass legislation prohibiting the practice and punishing its practitioners. But this necessary step is not enough to end the practice. Communities need to be made aware of the serious chronic and life-long health risks of the procedure and the lack of justification for such a damaging practice. In Niger, UNICEF has been working with a committee to change social practices through educating community members and providing them with knowledge and skills. The Niamey community in Niger has publicly promised to end female genital mutilation, and it has asked practitioners to "put down the knife." As a result, Haissa has become aware of the damaging consequences of female genital mutilation. To make it easier for her to give up her trade, she has learned gardening and has obtained a piece of land so that she can support her family financially. After understanding how damaging female genital mutilation can be to a girl's health, she stopped performing the procedure and is now "proud of starting a new life."[66]

PROBLEM: FORCING CHILDREN INTO MARRIAGE

Another form of exploitative or abusive behavior is child marriage. Child marriage is common in Bangladesh. Although the legal age for marriage is 18, almost half of all girls are married when they are 15. The parents of Mosamad Mounjera Khatun arranged for her to be married when she was 14.

Economic reasons play a role in parents' decisions to arrange marriages for their young girls. Marrying off a girl can ease the family's burden to support and feed her and help the rest of the family to survive. Other reasons for child marriage are based on unacceptable ideas of behavior that are considered proper for a married woman. Young girls are likely to be more obedient and submissive to their husbands, and they are more likely to have children. At the same time, child marriage denies a girl the opportunity to get an education, since after marriage young girls tend not to go to school. Child marriage also may lead to health problems. Pregnancies at a very young age may endanger the life of the mother or the baby. Teenage girls are susceptible to diseases such as HIV/AIDS that are passed on during sexual intercourse. Should a girl refuse to go along with an arranged marriage, she is likely to be punished. Girls who disobey their parents' wishes may even be killed in so-called "honor killings."

UNICEF'S RESPONSE

Based on research showing that more education prevents child marriage, UNICEF works to promote girls' education. With the support of UNICEF, a program in Bangladesh aims to give girls "a say in their own future."[67] The Kishori Abhijan project—which means "adolescent's journey" in Bangla—creates an environment supportive of these girls' right to participate in decisions about their lives. Rather than getting married at age 14, Mosamad wished to continue with school. With the help of her friends in the project, Mosamad called off her arranged marriage. Peer counselors finally convinced Mosamad's parents that allowing Mosamad to continue with school would enhance

Marriage at or shortly after puberty is common in many regions, such as sub-Saharan Africa, South Asia, and other parts of Asia. In parts of West and East Africa and areas of South Asia, marriages earlier than puberty are not unusual. UNICEF works to educate communities about the harmful consequences of child marriage and offers counseling and educational services to empower girls. Above, eight-year-old Mangilal with his wife Mangi, 7, leave a temple after getting married in central India.

her chances of finding work; ultimately her parents could also benefit from this decision.

PROBLEM: UNREGISTERED CHILDREN

Proof of age is essential to protect children from child marriage, child labor, and other forms of abuse and exploitation, but the births of many children are never registered. In 2003, 36 percent of all the world's estimated births went unregistered. Since there is no record of the births of up to 50 million children, there is no recognition of their legal identity.[68] Children whose births are not registered do not have access to basic services such as health care and immunization. Many are not enrolled in school at the right age. Even when they are older, they cannot get a passport, open a bank account, get a driver's license, or qualify for financial credit. They remain invisible to all efforts to protect them from various forms of abuse and exploitation such as child labor, underage military service, or child marriage. Ultimately, a lack of legal identity deprives children of citizenship, of rights to public office, and of financial well-being.

UNICEF'S RESPONSE

How do you help millions of children whose legal identity is not known because there is no documentation of their birth? Every government should officially record the birth of a child. Nonetheless, even if a government provides this essential free service and makes it compulsory, many parents in remote areas or in urban slums are ignorant of the benefits that their children might get from having their births registered. In Kolkata, India, UNICEF supported an initiative to award birth certificates to 50,000 street children and youths from underprivileged neighborhoods. Birth certificates will make it easier for these children to have access to health care and education. Having their births registered also will help protect the street children from potential abuse. Yet, many births remain unregistered, especially those of children born to extremely poor and uneducated families. Millions of people still need information about the procedures and usefulness of birth registration. UNICEF continues to support efforts to obtain birth certificates for unregistered children: the first necessary step to make every child in Kolkata count.

THE FUTURE

The goals that the world leaders set out to achieve for the millennium—such as children's health and education—cannot be achieved unless children are protected. Violence and abuse harm children's health and make it harder for them to concentrate, to learn, and even to attend schools. Child labor injures a child's health, jeopardizes education, and leads to further exploitation and abuse. Children who are abandoned or separated from their parents may have to work, to live in squalor and illness, and to give up their education. Female genital mutilation can cause health problems or even death. Child marriage usually means the end of a young girl's education. It may also endanger the health of a young mother or the health of a baby born to a very young mother. Armed conflict has a devastating impact on children's survival. Serving in the armed forces can disrupt children's education and make it very hard for them to assimilate back into their societies. Without an official record of birth, a child does not have access to services such as health and education.

UNICEF supports the creation of a protective environment for all children. To ensure children's survival, growth, and development, it is essential that governments, organizations, communities, and families work together toward this goal. Failing to protect children from violence and abuse squanders the world's most valuable resource and threatens the future.

Rights for All Children

Are we guilty of heartlessness? Lack of compassion? Let us call it a lack of imagination. We, today, love our children; but we are more or less indifferent to other people's children, especially if they are far away. Since we cannot see them, we fail to imagine them as they are somewhere else, on the other side, always on the other side: weak and frail, capable of tenderness and vulnerable to pain, ready to receive anything: to discover anything, to return fivefold anything that is given to them. If we are incapable of seeing all children as our own, we will never have anything more than hope.[69]

—Elie Wiesel, "Crimes Against Childhood" in *We the Children*

INTERNATIONAL CONVENTION
ON CHILDREN'S RIGHTS

On November 20, 1989, the UN General Assembly adopted the Convention on the Rights of the Child (CRC). This agreement says that all children under age 18 are entitled to the same rights. Then individual governments had to ratify the Convention to give it legal force. The ratifications came fast. A few months after the Convention was adopted, 20 countries already had ratified it. Within a decade, the CRC became the most widely ratified international human rights agreement in the world. Individual governments committed themselves to protecting and ensuring children's rights. Only two countries— Somalia and the United States—have yet to ratify the agreement, although both have signed it, indicating their support.

What rights does this agreement promise? First of all, it promises the same rights for all children, whatever their nationality, residence, sex, ethnicity, color, religion, or language. All children everywhere in the world are entitled to the same rights. This promise is a step toward the perspective that all children are as valuable as our own, or at least we recognize the value of all children. It is often difficult to reach out beyond the confines of the family, the neighborhood, the town, or the country and recognize that all children are valuable. But this recognition is necessary to make sure that some children are not denied the rights that the CRC promises.

Although the Convention spells out many different rights of children—health, education, an adequate standard of living, leisure and play, protection from exploitation, and expression of their own opinions—it stands for four basic principles. First, there should be no discrimination. No child should benefit or suffer because of race, color, gender, language, religion, origin, or disability. Second, laws and actions affecting children should put children's best interests first. Third, governments must protect children and ensure their survival and full development—physically, spiritually, morally, and socially. And

In 2007, the Convention on the Rights of the Child (CRC) celebrated 18 years of existence with the publication of *18 Candles*. This booklet of 18 articles is written by high-level officials and children's rights activists as well as children who express what the CRC means to them. Jean Zermatten, vice chair of the Committee on the Rights of the Child, holds up a copy of *18 Candles* during a press conference.

fourth, children have a right to participate in decisions that affect them and to have their opinions taken into account.

Since the adoption of the CRC, UNICEF has integrated children's rights into its mission statement, which states:

> UNICEF is guided by the Convention on the Rights of the Child and strives to establish children's rights as enduring ethical principles and international standards of behaviour towards children.[70]

Some of the rights in the Convention correspond with needs that formed the focus of UNICEF's work, even before the adoption of the CRC. Long before Article 24 of the CRC mentioned the right to health care, UNICEF had been working to provide preventive health care and to avert the deaths of infants and children. Before Article 28 affirmed the right to education, UNICEF had tried to make primary education available to all children. After the adoption of the CRC, UNICEF expanded its programs to cover additional aspects of child well-being such as protecting children from exploitation and abuse and ensuring equal treatment of boys and girls. UNICEF is actively involved with the Committee on the Rights of the Child, the body that examines each government's progress in ensuring that children have the rights as promised in the Convention. Before the committee meets, UNICEF submits country reports showing both steps forward and weaknesses in making rights real.

For much of the past, rights for children were virtually unheard of. Some states had laws to protect animals from cruelty before they had legislation to protect children from abuse. In 1646, the State of Massachusetts enacted the Stubborn Child Statute, which said that a stubborn or rebellious son above 15 years of age could be put to death if his parents had serious complaints. In 1874, parents were prosecuted in New York City for keeping their daughter chained to a bed and feeding her only bread and water. Because there was no law to protect children, the prosecutors had to argue that the child deserved protection in the same way that animals were worthy of protection against cruelty.[71]

Before the 1600s in Western Europe, children were not really seen as different from adults, at least not after early childhood. There was little attention paid to children as types of people distinct from adults. Children were put to work as soon as they were old enough. Boys farmed or hunted; girls cooked and cleaned. Not until the 1600s did children begin to appear in paintings of the time in dress and general demeanor looking different from the adults.

Yet children were not spared hard labor. After the start of the Industrial Revolution in the 1740s, children worked very long hours in dark factories without fresh air. In the United States, among the worst work environments for children were the coal mines in Pennsylvania. For up to 11 hours a day, small boys sitting on wooden boards had to bend over chutes through which coal flowed to pick out slate, stone, or other waste. The beginning of the twentieth century brought a movement in the United States to reduce child labor. The National Child Labor Committee, which was formed in 1904, started to gather information on the worst forms of child labor. It appealed to the conscience of the public to stop sacrificing children's lives for the sake of mining coal or manufacturing. The belief developed that children, distinct from adults, have certain rights.[72]

THE CHALLENGES

Today, the international community recognizes many rights of the child, but that does not mean that all children actually have the benefit of those rights in their lives. The demands of survival, lack of public funds and resources, and tradition may all deny children rights. The Convention means that governments must strive and work out the best ways to secure rights for children living in their territory, balancing resources with rights and rights against each other.

THE CONVENTION ON THE RIGHTS OF THE CHILD AND RIGHTS TO EDUCATION

As mentioned, the right to education is central to the development of the individual girl or boy. It is also central to the development of societies. Education can protect a child from many dangers such as living a life in lasting poverty, working unsafe jobs in agriculture or industry, performing domestic work for others without any prospect of advancement, or worse, serving as a child soldier in a war. Education also helps societies because educated citizens are better able to participate in policy and to think critically. Hopefully, they also are able to better understand the values of peace and of the dignity of every person. Yet, a right to an education appears to be an empty dream for children who work long hours inside or outside the home.

Twelve-year-old Joe[73] lives in London with his parents and grandmother. Because his parents work full-time, they are unable to take care of his grandmother, who is ill. They tell Joe to stay home from school to take care of his grandmother. Is this fair, particularly when the CRC says every child has a right to education? No, certainly not. Joe's parents, with the help of the government, should find a different caretaker for Joe's grandmother.

Long hours of work make it hard for 17-year-old Flor[74] in San Salvador to further her education. She struggles to complete fifth grade while working 13 hours a day as a domestic worker. She gets up at 2 A.M. every morning and starts work at 4:30 A.M., doing tasks such as washing, ironing, and taking care of children. For her hours of hard work she gets paid only 225 *colones* (about $26) each month. After work she attends a fifth-grade evening class at a night school, which is designed for children who work during the day. She usually gets home at 8 P.M., has dinner, and is then able to sleep about five hours. Like many other girls, Flor's work as a domestic servant interferes with her education, in violation of the CRC. She is able to attend night classes, but traveling to and from school at night carries risks to her safety. Her work sometimes interferes with her schooling when she has no time to do homework, falls asleep during class, or misses a day of school. According to Article 32(1), the Convention on the Rights of the Child prohibits economic exploitation and the employment of children in work that is likely to be hazardous, interfere with their education, or be harmful to their health or development.

What strategies can be used to ensure that children such as Flor have access to basic and secondary education and have enough time to study? Well, the government can limit the hours

Article 14 of the Convention of the Rights of the Child states that children have the right to practice their religion, as long as they are not stopping others from enjoying their rights. More schools have become more sensitive to religious issues, such as allowing Muslim students to pray, as long as it doesn't interfere with learning. Above, in a school in Denpasar, in Bali, Indonesia, Muslim students pray in their classroom.

that any child under 18 may work, punish those who violate the ban against child labor, and provide a stipend to compensate for income lost when children attend school.

When the right to education conflicts with another right, such as religion, the challenge is to find a compromise. Fifteen-year-old Annie[75] is an observant Muslim. According to Islamic law, she has to pray at specific times every day, regardless of whether she is in the middle of classes at school. It is possible to argue that Annie's right to education means she should not miss parts of the curriculum, but she should still be learning the same materials as other children. How can the right to education be reconciled with her right to religion? One possible compromise would be for the teacher to speak to Annie and her parents to make some kind of arrangement, such as asking her to catch up at the end of classes and to do the work she missed.

THE CONVENTION ON THE RIGHTS OF THE CHILD AND RIGHTS TO HEALTH

Every day more than 30,000 children under age five die of preventable causes and many more suffer from illnesses. Without life and health, any other rights are meaningless. The CRC recognizes that every child has the right to life (Article 6) and the right to "the highest attainable standard of health," as well as access to facilities for treatment and rehabilitation (Article 24).

Children in densely populated inner cities face challenges to their health. Peter[76] lives next door to drug dealers. When he steps out the front door of his small apartment, the passage is filled with dirty needles. His mother has complained to local government agencies about the situation, but they have not done anything. Should Peter and his family have to put up with the mess and the dangers to their health? No. According to Article 24, the right to health care extends to a clean and safe environment. The CRC also requires governments to use all means possible to protect children from the use of harmful drugs (Article 33).

A 2007 report from UNICEF said the United States and Great Britain were the worst countries in the industrialized world in which to be a child. The United States fared worst of all 21 countries in health and safety, measured by rates of infant mortality and accidents and injuries. The lone star state of Texas tops the nation with the number of children who have no health insurance.[77] Kristin Smith, 13, is one of them. Her mother, Tammy, a single parent, is a part-time postal carrier who is on a waiting list for a full-time job. She does not earn very much. Yet her income is just over the limit that would have qualified Kristin for free health care under federally funded and state-funded children's health insurance programs. Kristin has not seen a doctor in more than three years, and her mother is just praying that she will not get sick.

MAJOR REMAINING CHALLENGES

In 1991, the year after nearly every country had signed the CRC, politicians agreed on a plan for turning the Convention's words into reality. A decade later, UN secretary general Kofi Annan reported that children's health and education had improved, that there was more awareness of child abuse, and that countries across the world were making children a higher priority. Still, major challenges remain.

Despite improvements made since the 1990 World Summit, many children below age five still die needlessly, many children do not have enough food to eat, and many children are not attending school. Annan said the "unfulfilled commitments" at the beginning of the twenty-first century show how much still needs to be done to ensure the rights of every child.[78] As examples of human suffering, he mentioned that nearly 11 million children still die each year before their fifth birthday, many from causes that are preventable. Child survival has been set back by the spread of HIV/AIDS, especially in African countries south of the Sahara. The disease has caused millions of children to become orphans. About 150 million children are underfed, and about 120 million are out of school, most of them girls. Despite the hope that money would not be spent on wars, conflicts have continued to use up money that is necessary to save or improve children's lives.

Vast poverty is the biggest obstacle to making children's rights a reality. The evidence shows that children who grow up in poverty are more at risk. They are more likely to have health problems, to have learning and behavioral difficulties, to struggle in school, to have lower skills and ambitions, to work in low-paying jobs, or to be unemployed. While many children from low-income families do not fit these patterns, on average, children who grow up in poverty are at a disadvantage. Half of all people in the world are desperately poor, with 3 billion people living on less than $2 a day, and 1.2 billion barely surviving on less than $1 a day.[79] There is a huge gap between the average incomes of people in industrialized countries such as the United States, Canada, and Great Britain, and people in developing countries such as Indonesia, Kenya, and El Salvador. In the face of formidable obstacles, is there reason for guarded optimism that the rights of children like Joe, Flor, Annie, and Peter will be respected?

THE LIMITATIONS OF RIGHTS

The CRC's promises will probably make a difference in the lives of millions of children, but it does not promise to satisfy every desire or want. It promises respect for rights, which are not the same as wants. Human rights are rights to which all human beings are entitled, no matter what their age, culture, living circumstances, status in society, wealth or lack thereof. Every person or child has the right to have similar basic needs fulfilled such as nutritious food, health care, shelter, education, and protection from harm.

Wants are not protected because they are not usually essential for a child's survival, growth, and development. While every child has a need for a space to play and for recreation (Article 30), it is not essential that each child has a bicycle or takes regular holiday trips. While every child has a need for decent shelter (Article 27), each child does not need his or her own bedroom when growing up. While every child has the right to protection from abuse and neglect (Article 19), clothes in the latest style, while desirable, are not a basic need. While every child has a need for nutritious food and clean water (Article 24), fast food is not essential for survival and growth, and it may be even detrimental. While every child needs an education (Articles 28 and 29), a personal computer, television set, or MP3 player are mere wants that are not essential for development.

The CRC's promise of children's rights does not negate children's responsibilities. As part of their duties as citizens, children must learn to exercise their rights responsibly. Among the aims of education as defined in Article 29 are to encourage children to respect their parents, their own culture, and other cultures. Other articles emphasize that children must exercise their rights in a responsible way and with respect for the rights of others. Article 15, for example, mentions that children have the right to meet together and to join groups and organizations, as long as this does not stop others from enjoying their rights. Children have freedom to associate in voluntary organizations such as scouting, or campaigning for peace, or establishing a school union, but this right is not unlimited. Those who associate freely have to respect the rights of others to disagree or to form organizations with opposing goals.

The CRC recognizes the role of parents and the family to protect and care for children. Article 5, for example, states that governments should respect the rights and responsibilities of parents and families to direct and guide children. Article 18 respects parents' shared responsibility for bringing up their children and their duty to always consider what is best for each child. It also requires governments to help parents by providing support services, such as funding for public schools or special care for disabled children.

The CRC is not meant to grant children rights that would place them in conflict with parents and other figures of authority. Even though Article 12 gives children the right to say what should happen when adults make decisions that affect them, the intention of Article 12 is to encourage parents and other adults to listen to children's opinions and to involve them in decision making. The CRC's overriding goal is to encourage governments and every member of society to work together to

WHAT ARE YOUR RIGHTS?

The Convention on the Rights of the Child gives every child the right to live a safe and healthy life, with access to quality education and protection from abuse, exploitation, and violence. Some of your rights are listed below:

YOUR FAMILY

You have the right to know your parents and to be cared for by them to the extent possible. Both parents share responsibility for your upbringing, and they should consider what is best for each child. If your parents have separated, you have the right to stay in contact with both parents. Only if it is for your own good should you be separated from your parents—for example, when a parent mistreats or neglects you. If your own family cannot take care of you, you have the right to be looked after properly by people who respect your religion, culture, and language (Articles 7, 9, 18, 20).

YOUR FRIENDS AND YOUR FREE TIME

You have a right to relax and play, to meet with friends, and to join groups and organizations. You also have the right to join in a wide range of activities, such as playing sports, acting in a theater group, singing in a choir, taking dance lessons, or learning to play a musical instrument (Articles 15 and 31).

YOUR IDENTITY

You have the right to a name. You also have a right to be officially registered as a person so that you may get a driver's license, obtain a passport to travel, and as an adult, to get married. And you have a right to privacy. That means that a journalist cannot take a picture of you and publish it in a newspaper if you and your parents have not agreed to it (Articles 7, 8, 16).

YOUR SCHOOL

You have a right to education and a right not to be disciplined there without respecting your dignity. Primary education should be free. At school you should have the opportunity to develop your personality and talents. You should also learn to respect your parents and the cultures of others (Articles 28 and 29).

YOUR BELIEFS

With guidance from your parents, you have the right to think and believe what you want. If you are religious, you have the right to practice your religion, as long as you respect the religions of others (Article 14).

WORK

You are allowed to work, as long as the work is not dangerous or harmful to your health, education, or development. Helping around the house or tidying your room is certainly permitted (Articles 32 and 36.).

FOOD, WATER, AND HEALTH CARE

To stay healthy, you have the right to clean water, nutritious food, a clean environment, and good quality health care. If you are disabled, you have the right to special care and support. Rich countries should help poorer countries to achieve this (Articles 23 and 24).

THE LAW

If you have done something wrong and are accused of breaking the law, you have the right to receive legal help. You should not be treated cruelly, and you should only go to prison for the most

(continues)

(continued)

serious offenses. Even then, you should not be put in prison with adults, and you should be able to keep contact with your family (Articles 37 and 40).

WARS AND VIOLENCE

If a war breaks out, you should receive special protection. Nobody under 15 should be allowed to join the army (Article 38).

FINDING INFORMATION

You have the right to find information on the Internet. That does not mean that your dad cannot forbid you from playing a computer game that is certified for older children or from visiting certain Web sites that may be damaging to you. You can also get information from television, the radio, or newspapers. This information should be given in language that you can readily understand, and it should not be harmful to you or other children (Articles 13 and 17).

SPEAKING YOUR MIND

You should have a say when adults make decisions about you. You also have the right to say, draw, or write what you want, as long as the information does not hurt other people (Articles 12 and 13).

create an environment in which children can develop their full potential, free from hunger, neglect, and abuse.

Governments make rights real by passing laws, adopting policies, taking action, and making funding available for children's programs. The Armenian government has passed laws to make sure that there is no discrimination against refugee children. Germany has continued to work on reducing racism and dislike of foreigners. In Vietnam, the Ministry of Justice has implemented an appropriate judicial process for young people, and it has trained judges, police, and other legal professionals in dealing with juveniles who commit offenses.

Governments have the main responsibility to make sure that rights are respected. They have to pass laws to transform the standards into reality for all children, and they have to allocate the necessary funds. Governments have to report periodically to the Committee on the Rights of the Child, a committee of independent experts, on the status of children's rights in their countries. UNICEF and other UN agencies regularly read the reports and prepare questions for the committee's formal meetings. If a country violates the Convention, the CRC will report on violations. Along with public criticism by other countries and organizations, the CRC reports put pressure on countries to change the way they treat children.

The main reason that the CRC will actually make a difference in the lives of children is that the world knows what needs to be done to guarantee the rights and well-being of children. Providing education, improving health care, respecting religion, and supplying safe water and adequate nutrition do not require sophisticated technical knowledge or very large sums of money. Ensuring rights mainly requires adjusting priorities in the spending of both poorer and wealthier countries. Poorer countries need to spend less on defense and more on essential social services such as basic education, nutrition, and basic health care. Wealthier nations, which spend about 10 times more on defense than on international aid for developing countries, need to adjust their budgets to make sure that more aid goes toward development assistance. The UN has estimated that if 22 rich countries give 0.7 percent of their gross national income to assist poorer nations, poverty can be largely wiped out by 2025. The United States now spends considerably less on development aid—about 0.15 percent of its GDP.[80] To be most effective in tackling poverty and promoting development, investments must be targeted at schools, clinics, safe water and sanitation, electricity, roads, and transport to get goods to markets. Compared to what countries spend on wars, weapons, or luxury consumer goods, only modest resources are needed to provide for basic needs of children. The CRC provides a framework and a vision of children's rights on which there is wide agreement. Now it is up to government leaders and other individuals in societies to make sure that there is the political will to change national priorities and to invest in the well-being of children.

UNICEF: Progress and Challenges

IN 1950 THE INTERNATIONAL CHILDREN'S EMERGENCY FUND (ICEF), which had been created to deal with the short-term emergency after World War II, was scheduled to close. The delegate from Pakistan to the UN General Assembly convinced the Assembly that the organization was still vital. Speaking from the perspective of one of the new nations of the developing world, he asked how the task of international action for children could be regarded as complete when so many millions of children in Asia, Africa, and Latin America suffered from sickness and hunger, not because of war but because of poverty. After his striking plea, the UN General Assembly confirmed UNICEF's permanent status in 1953. UNICEF became one of the lasting islands in the UN archipelago.

Above, mothers in Amritsar, India, wait at a clinic for their children to be administered the DPT (diphtheria, pertussis, and tetanus) vaccine. According to UNICEF, 22 percent of 11 million global child deaths and 30 percent of global neonatal deaths occur in India, mainly from 6 largely preventable causes, namely, pneumonia, diarrhea, malaria, neonatal pneumonia, preterm delivery, and asphyxia. UNICEF has been a global leader in vaccine supply, reaching 40 percent of the world's children.

Half a century later, in September 2000, when the largest group of world leaders in history gathered in New York for the Millennium Summit, it became clear that the world still had an indispensable need for UNICEF. Many children in developing countries, and some in the world's richest countries, continued to suffer under conditions of severe poverty, brutal conflict, and a degraded environment. The 189 member states of the UN agreed on a set of goals to be achieved by 2015—the Millennium Development Goals.

As the only intergovernmental agency within the UN devoted exclusively to children, UNICEF has an important role to play in achieving these goals. Six of the eight goals concern children directly: doing away with extreme poverty and hunger; achieving primary education for all children; promoting equality of girls and boys; reducing children's deaths; improving mothers' health; and fighting diseases such as HIV/AIDS and malaria. The other two goals, protecting the environment and developing partnerships between rich and poor countries to help development, also seek to improve children's lives. Although UNICEF plays an important role in attaining all eight goals as they apply to children, a key goal is Millennium Development Goal 4: to reduce by two-thirds the number of deaths among children under the age of five. The target date for this goal is 2015. UNICEF executive director Ann Veneman has said, "In order to do that we really have to figure out what works and how to measure the results."[81]

UNICEF already has figured out that a strong grassroots presence in communities is necessary to lead the fight against child mortality. In a country such as Ghana, UNICEF has helped to strengthen community-based health systems. With UNICEF's aid, communities have worked together to make sure there is a supply of clean water, good nutrition for mothers as well as for children, and immunizations for children. Community programs were created to train mothers how to deal with children's diseases. These programs have successfully reduced the number of deaths among young children.

Still, communities cannot bring about lasting improvements without government support. The most effective way to make sure that governments pay attention to and commit resources for children is to demand that governments respect children's rights. In many countries, UNICEF and other organizations have used the Convention on the Rights of the Child as a tool to guide government policies and programs and to ensure that children's rights are protected. In Egypt, the government has changed the law to recognize the right of every child to be raised in a family environment. In Burkina Faso, new legislation requires children to attend school until at least age 16. The Romanian government has changed the law to prohibit corporal punishment. Sri Lanka has raised the minimum age for employment from 12 to 14 years. As governments have taken meaningful steps to make children's rights concrete, children's lives have visibly changed.

The CRC provides principles and standards that can guide federal, state, and local governments to deal with difficulties that children encounter and to strengthen families. Every self-governing nation in the world has ratified the Convention on the Rights of the Child, with one major exception—the United States (Somalia also has not ratified the CRC, but they have no permanent national government). Many children in the United States face considerable difficulties. More infants in the United States die than in most other industrialized countries. Many children lack adequate health care and educational opportunities. Many children live in poverty and hunger. Almost 10,000 minors in the United States are held in adult jails and prisons, where they are likely to become victims of abuse due to their size and youth.[82] Too many children die as a result of the inappropriate use of firearms.

The United States' failure to ratify the CRC means that the Convention has no legal force within the country. It also means that the United States does not take part in evaluating and advising other nations on how they treat their children. Ratification of the CRC by the United States would add a strong voice to help ensure that the world protects and promotes the health, welfare, and security of children.

In 1990, the UN offered a wonderful gift to the world's children: The Convention on the Rights of the Child. This gift has accumulated promises from 193 countries to respect and protect children, to listen to them, and to allow them to live and to grow. Even though the state of the world shows that the

Children played with a ball that symbolizes the world at a UNICEF meeting in Berlin, Germany, on May 16, 2001. Around the world, children, governments, and nonprofit groups came together to talk about the rights of children. The results of a Young Voices poll of more than 93 million children from 35 countries reflected the deep conviction that young people must be considered on matters that affect them and their voices must be heard by those shaping the world they will inherit.

promises of the CRC are hard to keep, the CRC is a valuable guide in the struggle to protect children's rights. The failure of the United States to ratify the Convention makes it impossible for the country to be a leader in respecting children's rights and bringing about positive change.

In a changing world, it is good to know that there is a trusted "brand name" that is working for children everywhere.

UNICEF is present, even in remote corners of the world; it is known everywhere; and it has a track record of knowledge, credibility, and respect. UNICEF depends on us and on the rest of the world to join in its commitment to the well-being and the best interests of children, as well as the protection of their human rights. As South Africa's Nobel Peace Prize winner Archbishop Desmond M. Tutu has said, "We each can make a difference if we are vigilant to create a new kind of society, more compassionate, more caring, more sharing where human rights, where children's rights are respected and protected. Politicians ultimately offer what the people want. Let us tell them we want peace and prosperity for everyone. Start today."[83]

CHRONOLOGY

1945 World War II ends.

1946 The United Nations (UN) creates the International
      Children's Emergency Fund (ICEF) to help children
      in Europe after World War II.

1950 The United Nations General Assembly votes to
      expand ICEF's role.

1953 UNICEF drops the words *International* and *Emergency*
      from its title. It becomes simply the United Nations
      Children's Fund, while retaining its well-known
      acronym, UNICEF.

1959 The UN General Assembly adopts the Declaration of
      the Rights of the Child.

1960 Mother and child symbol replaces the old UNICEF
      emblem of a child with a cup of milk.

1965 UNICEF receives the Nobel Peace Prize.

1979 UNESCO declares it the International Year of the Child.

1982 UNICEF launches the "child survival and
      development revolution." It promotes the formula
      known as GOBI: Growth monitoring, Oral
      rehydration, Breastfeeding, and Immunization.

1985 Civil war in El Salvador is halted for three days—"days
      of tranquility"—to allow children to be vaccinated.

1989 The UN General Assembly adopts the Convention on
      the Rights of the Child.

1990 The World Summit for Children, a gathering of
      government leaders, takes place at UN headquarters
      in New York City.

1996   UNICEF supports an important study, "The Impact of Armed Conflict on Children."

2000   UN adopts the Millennium Development Goals.

2005   UNICEF and its partners launch the global campaign, "Unite for Children. Unite against AIDS."

NOTES

Introduction

1. Daniel Defoe, *Robinson Crusoe*. New York: W. W. Norton & Co., 1975, 11.
2. Marc Lacey, "Hurricane Ike Smashes West Through Caribbean," *New York Times*, September 7, 2008. Available online at *http://www.nytimes.com/2008/09/08/world/americas/08ike.html*.
3. Jasmine Pittinger, "Delivering Life-saving Aid to Hurricane-affected Children and Families in Haiti," UNICEF. Available online at *http://www.unicef.org/info bycountry/haiti_45659.html*.
4. Elizabeth Kiem, "Goodwill Ambassador Mia Farrow Urges Tsunami-like Response in Haiti's Disaster Zones," UNICEF. Available online at *http://www.unicef.org/info bycountry/haiti_45708.html*.
5. Elizabeth Kiem, "Haiti's Flood-damaged Schools Struggle to Reopen," UNICEF. Available online at *http://www. unicef.org/infobycountry/haiti_45837.html*.

Chapter One: Improving the Lives of Children

6. Unicef Slogan. Available online at *http://www.unicef.org/ advsearch.html*.
7. Maggie Black, *The Children and the Nations*, South Melbourne: Macmillan,1987,12.
8. Victor Chinyama, "Kenya's Abolition of School Fees Offers Lessons for Rest of Africa," UNICEF. Available online at *http://www.unicef.org/infobycountry/kenya_33391.html*.
9. Kun Li, "Goodwill Ambassador Sarah Jessica Parker Helps Launch 'Trick-or-Treat for UNICEF'," UNICEF. Available online at *http://www.unicef.org/infobycountry/ usa_36347.html*.

10. "Procuring Supplies for Children: Vaccines," UNICEF. Available online at *http://www.unicef.org/supply/index_polio.html*.

11. "UNICEF Leadership 2005–2015: A Call for Strategic Change," *The Lancet*, Volume 364, Issue 9451, 2071–2074.

12. Thomas Nybo, "Ann M. Veneman Is First UNICEF Executive Director to Visit Swaziland," UNICEF. Available online at *http://www.unicef.org/infobycountry/swaziland_27142.html*.

13. Paula Harrington, "Lang Lang Launches Foundation to Support Children's Love of Music," UNICEF quoting the *New York Times*. Available online at *http://www.unicef.org/infobycountry/china_46066.html*.

14. "About UNICEF," UNICEF. Available online at *http://www.unicef.org/about/who/index_introduction.html*.

Chapter Two: The History of UNICEF

15. Presentation speech by Mrs. Aase Lionaes, Member of the Nobel Committee. Available online at *http://nobelprize.org/nobel_prizes/peace/laureates/1965/press.html*.

16. Yves Beigbeder, *New Challenges for UNICEF*. New York: Palgrave, 2001, 12.

17. Maggie Black, *The Children and the Nations*, 19.

18. Judith M. Spiegelman and UNICEF, *We Are the Children*. Boston/New York: The Atlantic Monthly Press, 1986, 41, 48, 50.

19. Ibid.

20. "1946–2006: Sixty Years for Children," UNICEF, 22. Available online at *http://www.unicef.org/publications/files/1946-2006_Sixty_Years_for_Children.pdf*.

21. Maggie Black, *Children First*. New York: Oxford University Press, 1996, 91–96.

22. "The State of the World's Children 1987," UNICEF. Available online at *http://www.unicef.org/sowc/archive/ENGLISH/The%20State%20of%20the%20World%27s%20Children%201987.pdf.*

23. "Latin American Region Unites for Millions of 'Invisible' Children," UNICEF. Available online at *http://www.unicef.org/infobycountry/media_40731.html.*

24. "Amazon Sub-regional Programme—Peru, 2003–2007," UNICEF. Available online at *http://www.unicef.org/peru/_files/programacooperacion/peru_AmazonSubRegionalProg2003_2007.pdf.*

25. "The Meena Communication Initiative," UNICEF. Available online at *http://www.unicef.org/lifeskills/index_8021.html.*

26. "1946–2006: Sixty Years for Children," 27.

27. "The State of the World's Children 2008," 7.

28. "Basic Education and Gender Equality," UNICEF. Available online at *http://www.unicef.org/girlseducation/index_42997.html.*

29. "UN Finds Teen-Age Girls at High Risk of AIDS," *New York Times.* Available online. URL: *http://query.nytimes.com/gst/fullpage.html?sec=health&res=9F0CEEDA103CF933A05754C0A965958260.*

Chapter Three: Reducing Child Mortality

30. Foreword by Bono in Jeffrey D. Sachs, *The End of Poverty.* New York: Penguin Books, 2005.

31. "The State of the World's Children 1987," 1.

32. "Life Expectancy in Sub-Saharan Africa is Lower Now than 30 Years Ago: UN index," UN News Centre. Available online at *http://www.un.org/apps/news/story.asp?NewsID=20548&Cr=human&Cr1=develop.*

33. "The Impact of Infectious Diseases," Global Health Council. Available online at *http://www.globalhealth.org/infectious_diseases/*.

34. "Pneumonia: The Forgotten Killer of Children," UNICEF/WHO, 2006, 4.

35. "Remarks of Ann M. Veneman, Executive Director, UNICEF, Unite for Children, Unite Against AIDS." Launch Hour, October 25, 2005, New York, NY. Available online at *http://www.uniteforchildren.org/press/press_29410.htm*.

36. "Voices of Youth: Ogechi (17, Nigeria)," UNICEF. Available online at *http://www.unicef.org/voy/speakout/speakout_949.html*.

37. "Six Diseases Cause 90% of Infectious Disease Deaths," WHO. Available online at *http://www.who.int/infectious-disease-report/pages/ch2text.html#Anchor3*.

38. "Malnutrition's Effects," *The Economist*. Available online at *http://www.economist.com/world/international/displaystory.cfm?story_id=10566634*.

39. "Dietary Recommendations for Healthy Children," American Heart Association. Available online at *http://americanheart.org/presenter.jhtml?identifier=4575*. See also "Table: Dietary Recommendations for Children," AHA. Available online at *http://americanheart.org/presenter.jhtml?identifier=3033999*.

40. Judith M. Spiegelman and UNICEF, *We Are the Children*. New York: Atlantic Monthly Press, 1986, 174.

41. Ibid., 165.

42. Chris Niles, "UNICEF-supported Clinic Offers Hope to Those Living with HIV/AIDS in Lesotho," UNICEF. Available online at *http://www.unicef.org/infobycountry/lesotho_44323.html*.

Chapter Four: Basic Education for All

43. "The State of The World's Children 2004: Girls, Education and Development," UNICEF, vii. Available online at *http://www.unicef.org/sowc04/files/SOWC_O4_eng.pdf*.

44. "Basic Education and Gender Equality," UNICEF.

45. "The State of The World's Children 2004," 25.

46. Ibid.

47. Ibid., 31.

48. Ibid., 35.

49. Victor Chinyama, "Kenya's Abolition of School Fees Offers Lessons for Rest of Africa, UNICEF. Available online at *http://www.unicef.org/infobycountry/kenya_33391.html*.

50. "Clean Drinking Water and Separate Latrines Improve School Life for Girls and Boys in Afar Region," UNICEF. Available online at *http://www.unicef.org/ethiopia/ET_real_Afar_.pdf*. See also "Clean Water and Adequate Sanitation Keeping Children in School," UNICEF. Available online at *http://www.unicef.org/infobycountry/ethiopia_24128.html*.

51. Ibid.

52. "The State of The World's Children 2004," 61. Available online at *http://www.unicef.org/sowc/archive/ENGLISH/The%20State%20of%20the%20World%27s%20Children%202004.pdf*.

53. Ibid.

54. Ibid.

55. Bjørn lyngstad, "Life-skills Training Turns Turkmen Students into Pioneers of AIDS Awareness," UNICEF. Available online at *http://www.unicef.org/girlseducation/Turkmenistan_39838.html*.

56. "Millennium Development Goals—Goal: Achieve Universal Primary Education," UNICEF. Available online at *http://www.unicef.org/mdg/education.html*.

57. Ibid.

58. Carol Douglis, "First Lady of Rwanda Awards Young Women for their Scholastic Achievement," UNICEF. Available online at *http://www.unicef.org/infobycountry/ rwanda_43923.html.*

Chapter Five: Protecting Children from Violence and Abuse

59. Statement by Paulo Sérgio Pinheiro, "United Nations Secretary-General's Study on Violence against Children," United Nations General Assembly. Available online at *http://violencestudy.org/IMG/pdf/IE_Statement_GA-06.pdf.*

60. "Child Protection from Violence, Exploitation and Abuse: The Big Picture," UNICEF. Available online at *http://www.unicef.org/protection/index_bigpicture.html.*

61. Suzanna Dayne, "Justice and Support for Victims of Child Sexual Abuse in Indonesia," UNICEF. Available online at *http://www.unicef.org/protection/indonesia_40484.html.*

62. "Child Protection from Violence, Exploitation and Abuse: Child Labour," UNICEF. Available online at *http://www.unicef.org/protection/index_childlabour.html.*

63. "Project Aims to Ensure Education for Child Labourers in Drought-affected Ethiopia," UNICEF. Available online at *http://www.unicef.org/protection/ethiopia_44877.html.*

64. Mary de Sousa, "Lahore's Street Children Find Alternatives at UNICEF-supported Centre" UNICEF. Available online at *http://www.unicef.org/infobycountry/pakistan_ 36506.html.*

65. Joelle Onimus-Pfortner & Gaelle Bausson, "Turning Former Practitioners against Female Genital Mutilation in Niger," UNICEF. Available online at *http://www.unicef. org/protection/niger_44262.html.*

66. Ibid.

67. Steve Nettleton, "Empowering Girls by Challenging the Tradition of Child Marriage," UNICEF. Available online at *http://www.unicef.org/infobycountry/bangladesh_35505. html.*

68. "Factsheet: Birth Registration," UNICEF. Available online at *http://www.unicef.org/newsline/2003/03fsbirth registration.htm.*

Chapter Six: Rights for All Children

69. Elie Wiesel, "Crimes Against Childhood," in *We the Children.* New York: W. W. Norton, 1990, 26.

70. UNICEF Mission Statement. Available online at *http:// www.unicef.org/about/who/index_mission.html.*

71. UNICEF, *Protecting the World's Children.* New York: Cambridge University Press, 2007, 40.

72. Elaine Landau, *Your Legal Rights.* New York: Walker and Co., 1995, 7–13.

73. "Youthvoice Quiz," UNICEF. Available online at *http:// unicef.org.uk/youthvoice/personalityquiz.asp?quiz=2.*

74. "El Salvador: Abuses against Child Domestic Workers in El Salvador," Human Rights Watch, January 2004, Vol. 16, No. 1(B). Available online at *http://crin.org/docs/ resources/treaties/crc.36/El%20Salvador_HRW_ngo_ report(E).pdf.*

75. "Youthvoice Quiz," UNICEF.

76. "Kids Rights," DirectgovKids. Available online. URL: *http://kids.direct.gov.uk/resource_areas/html/games/kids_ rights.htm.*

77. "Texas Tops Nation in Number of Uninsured Children," Families USA. Available online at *http://familiesusa.org/ resources/newsroom/press-releases/2008-press-releases/ texas-tops-nation-in-number.html.* See also "Household

Income Rises, Poverty Rate Declines, Number of Uninsured Up," U.S. Census Bureau News. Available online
at *http://www.census.gov/Press-Release/www/releases/
archives/income_wealth/010583.html.*

78.   "We the Peoples: The Role of the United Nations in the
      Twenty-first Century, Report of the Secretary General,"
      United Nations General Assembly. Available online at
      *http://unpan1.un.org/intradoc/groups/public/documents/
      un/unpan000923.pdf.*

79.   Ibid.

80.   "Poverty Plan," PBS Online NewsHour with Jim Lehrer,
      January 17, 2005. Available online at *http://www.pbs.org/
      newshour/bb/international/jan-june05/poverty_1-17.html.*

Chapter Seven: UNICEF: Progress and Challenges

81.   Clare Kapp, "Ann Veneman: Getting UNICEF Back to
      Basics." *The Lancet*, Vol. 368, September 23, 2006, 1061.

82.   Carol Chodroff, "Reforming Juvenile Injustice," Human
      Rights Watch. Available online at *http://www.hrw.org/en/
      news/2008/07/01/reforming-juvenile-injustice.*

83.   Archbishop Desmond M. Tutu, "Forward," in "For Every
      Child," UNICEF. New York: Phyllis Fogelman Books, 2001.

BIBLIOGRAPHY

"Abuses Against Child Domestic Workers in El Salvador," Human Rights Watch, January 2004, Vol. 16, No. 1(B). Available online at http://www.crin.org/docs/resources/treaties/crc.36/El%20Salvador_HRW_ngo_report(E).pdf.

"Acceptance speech by Henry R. Labouisse, Executive Director of UNICEF, on the occasion of the award of the Nobel Peace Prize in Oslo," December 10, 1965. Available online at http://nobelprize.org/nobel_prizes/peace/laureates/1965/unicef-acceptance.html.

"A Devastating Hurricane Season Batters Haiti and the Caribbean," *New York Times*, September 10, 2008. Available online at http://query.nytimes.com/gst/fullpage.html?res=9F04E5DF1639F933A2575AC0A96E9C8B63.

Annan, Kofi A., United Nations Secretary-General. "We the Children: Meeting the Promises of the World Summit for Children," United Nations Secretary-General's Report, September 2001. Available online at http://www.unicef.org/specialsession/about/sgreport-pdf/sgreport_adapted_eng.pdf.

"At a Glance: Haiti," UNICEF. Available online at http://www.unicef.org/infobycountry/haiti_2014.html.

"Basic Education and Gender Equality," UNICEF. Available online at http://www.unicef.org/girlseducation/index_bigpicture.html.

Beigbeder, Yves. *New Challenges for UNICEF: Children, Women and Human Rights.* New York, NY: Palgrave, 2001.

Black, Maggie. *The Children and the Nations: Growing Up Together in the Postwar World.* South Melbourne, AU: Macmillan, 1987.

———. *Children First: The Story of UNICEF, Past and Present.* New York, NY: Oxford University Press, 1996.

Bonham Carter, Rachel. "A Former Child Soldier Speaks Out at UN Session on Challenges Facing Girls," UNICEF. Available online at http://www.unicef.org/protection/index_38532.html.

Castillo, Raul. "After the Storms: Field Diary from Flood-Stricken Gonaïves, Haiti," UNICEF. Available online at http://www.unicef.org/infobycountry/haiti_45806.html.

Castro, Juan Pablo. "New PSAs in Ecuador Urge Pregnant Women to be Tested and Treated for HIV," UNICEF. Available online at http://www.unicef.org/aids/ecuador_37956.html.

"Child Marriage," UNICEF. Available online at http://www.unicef.org/protection/index_earlymarriage.html.

"Child Poverty in Perspective: An Overview of Child Well-being in Rich Countries," UNICEF, Innocenti Research Center. Report Card 7, 2007. Available online at http://www.unicef.org/media/files/ChildPovertyReport.pdf.

"Child Protection from Violence, Exploitation and Abuse: The Big Picture," UNICEF. Available online at http://www.unicef.org/protection/index_bigpicture.html.

"Child Protection Information Sheets," UNICEF. Available online at http://www.unicef.org/protection/files/Child_Protection_Information_Sheets_(Booklet).pdf.

"Children without Parental Care," UNICEF. Available online at http://www.unicef.org/protection/index_orphans.html.

"Clean Drinking Water and Separate Latrines Improve School Life for Girls and Boys in Afar Region," UNICEF. Available online at http://www.unicef.org/ethiopia/ET_real_Afar_.pdf.

"Clean Water and Adequate Sanitation Keeping Children in School," UNICEF. Available online at http://www.unicef.org/infobycountry/Ethiopia_24128.html.

Dayne, Suzanna. "Justice and Support for Victims of Child Sexual Abuse in Indonesia," UNICEF. Available online at http://www.unicef.org/protection/Indonesia_40484.html.

Douglis, Carol. "First Lady of Rwanda Awards Young Women for Their Scholastic Achievements," UNICEF. Available online at http://www.unicef.org/infobycountry/Rwanda_43923.html.

"Education Statistics Version 5.3," Worldbank. Available online at http://www.worldbank.org/education/edstats.

"Food Is Not Enough: Without Essential Nutrients Millions of Children Will Die," Doctors without Borders. Available online at http://www.doctorswithoutborders.org/news/malnutrition/FoodIsNotEnough.pdf.

Harrington, Paula. "Lang Lang Launches Foundation to Support Children's Love of Music," UNICEF. Available online at http://www.unicef.org/infobycountry/china_46066.html.

"Investing in Development," UN Millennium Project. Available online at http://www.unmillenniumproject.org/reports/index.htm.

Kapp, Clare. "Ann Veneman: Getting UNICEF Back to Basics," *The Lancet*, Vol. 368, September 23, 2006, p. 1061.

Kiem, Elizabeth. "Goodwill Ambassador Mia Farrow Urges Tsunami-like Response in Haiti's Disaster Zones," UNICEF. Available online at http://www.unicef.org/infobycountry/Haiti_45708.html.

———. "Haiti's Flood-Damaged Schools Struggle to Reopen," UNICEF. Available online at http://www.unicef.org/infobycountry/Haiti_45837.html.

Lacey, Marc. "Hurricane Ike Smashes West Through Caribbean," *New York Times*, September 7, 2008. Available online at http://www.nytimes.com/2008/09/08/world/americas08ike.html?partner=rssnyt.

Landau, Elaine. *Your Legal Rights: From Custody Battles to School Searches, the Headline-making Cases that Affect Your Life*. New York, NY: Walker & Co., 1995.

"Life Skills Introduction," UNICEF. Available online at http://www.unicef.org/lifeskills/index.html.

Lyngstad, Bjørn. "Life-skills Training Turns Turkmen Students into Pioneers of AIDS Awareness," UNICEF. Available online at http://www.unicef.org/girlseducation/Turkmenistan_39838.html.

"Malnutrition," Doctors without Borders. Available online at http://www.doctorswithoutborders.org/news/malnutrition/background.cfm.

"Management of Pneumonia in Community Settings," WHO and UNICEF Joint Statement, August 2004. Available online at http://www.unicef.org/publications/files/EN_Pneumonia_reprint.pdf.

"Millennium Development Goals: About," UNICEF. Available online at http://www.unicef.org/mdg/28184_28230.htm.

"Millennium Development Goals," UNICEF. Available online at http://www.unicef.org/mdg/index.html.

"Millennium Development Goals: Achieve Universal Primary Education," UNICEF. Available online at http://www.unicef.org/mdg/education.html.

Nettleton, Steve. "Empowering Girls by Challenging the Tradition of Child Marriage," UNICEF. Available online at http://www.unicef.org/infobycountry/Bangladesh_35505.html.

Nybor, Thomas. "Ann M. Veneman Is First UNICEF Executive Director to Visit Swaziland," UNICEF. Available online at http://www.unicef.org/infobycountry/Swaziland_27142.html.

O'Connor, Anahad. "Hurricane Heads for Haiti," *New York Times*, August 27, 2008. Available online at http://www.nytimes.com/2008/08/27/world/Americas/27Haiti.html.

"On CRC anniversary, Ishmael Beah Appointed UNICEF Advocate for Children Affected by War," UNICEF. Available online at http://www.unicef.org/protection/index_41894.html.

Onimus-Pfortner, Joelle & Gaelle Bausson. "Turning Former Practitioners Against Female Genital Mutilation in Niger," UNICEF. Available online at http://www.unicef.org/protection/niger_44262.html.

"Pakistan's Children Say to President: Please Do More for Education," UNICEF. Available online at http://www.unicef.org/infobycountry/Pakistan_24504.html.

Perlmutt, Bent Jorgen. "Maisha's Story: Former Child Soldier Reclaims His Life in DR Congo," UNICEF. Available online at http://www.unicef.org/protection/drcongo_41224.html.

———. "Masika's Story: Child Combatant in DR Congo Recalls the Emptiness of Army Life," UNICEF. Available online at http://www.unicef.org/protection/drcongo_41183.html.

Pittenger, Jasmine. "Delivering Life-saving Aid to Hurricane-affected Children and Families in Haiti," UNICEF. Available online at http://www.unicef.org/infobycountry/Haiti_45659.html.

"Pneumonia: The Forgotten Killer of Children," UNICEF and the World Health Organization, 2006. Available online at http://www.unicef.org/publications/index_35626.html.

"Presentation Speech by Mrs. Aase Lionaes, Member of the Nobel Committee," Nobel Peace Prize 1965. Available online at http://nobelprize.org/nobel_prizes/peace/laureates/1965/press.html.

"Project Aims to Ensure Education for Child Laborers in Drought-affected Ethiopia," UNICEF. Available online at http://www.unicef.org/protection/Ethiopia_44877.html.

"Protecting and Supporting Children Affected by HIV and AIDS," UNICEF. Available online at http://www.unicef.org/aids/index_armedconflict.html.

"Remarks of Ann M. Veneman, Executive Director, UNICEF, Unite for Children, Unite Against AIDS." Launch Hour,

October 25, 2005. Available online at http://www.unitefor
children.org/press/press_29410.htm.

"Rights, Wants & Needs," UNICEF Canada. Available online
at http://www.unicef.ca/portal/Secure/Community/502/
WCM/EDUCATION/assets/pdf/EngRightsKit02.pdf.

de Sousa, Mary. "Lahore's Street Children Find Alternatives at
UNICEF-supported Centre," UNICEF. Available online at
http://www.unicef.org/infobycountry/Pakistan_36506.html.

"Special Feature: Saving Lives in an Abandoned Land," Doctors
without Borders, September 9, 2005. Available online at http://
www.doctorswithoutborders.org/news/article.cfm?id=1588.

Spiegelman, Judith M. and UNICEF. *We Are the Children: A
Celebration of UNICEF's First Forty Years.* Boston, MA/New
York, NY: The Atlantic Monthly Press, 1986.

"Storm Surge Left 500 Dead in Haiti," *New York Times*, September 5, 2008. Available online at http://www.nytimes.
com/2008/09/06/world/americas/06haiti.html?ref=americas.

"Summary Report: Study on the Impact of the Implementation
of the Convention on the Rights of the Child," UNICEF Innocenti Research Centre. Available online at http://www.unicef-
irc.org/publications/pdf/CRC_Impact_summaryreport.pdf.

"The Campaign for U.S. Ratification of the Convention on the
Rights of the Child (CRC)." 2008. Available online at http://
childrightscampaign.org/documents/InformationPacket.pdf.

"Treating Malnutrition: We Can Do It, but Where Is the Will
to Act?" Doctors without Borders. AccessNews, March
2008, No. 17. Available online at http://doctorswithoutbor-
ders.org/news/malnutrition/AccessNewNutrition.pdf.

UNICEF. *1946-2006 Sixty Years for Children: A State of the
World's Children Special Report.* New York, NY: UNICEF.
Available online at http://www.unicef.org/publications/
files/1946-2006_Sixty_Years_for_Children.pdf.

———. "Annual Report 2006." Available online at http://www. unicef.org/publications/files/Annual_Report_2006.pdf.

———. *For Every Child: The UN Convention on the Rights of the Child in Words and Pictures.*" New York, NY: Phyllis Fogelman Books, 2001. Foreword by Archbishop Desmond M. Tutu.

———. *Protecting the World's Children: Impact of the Convention on the Rights of the Child in Diverse Legal Systems.* New York, NY: Cambridge University Press, 2007.

———. "The State of the World's Children 1987." Available online at http://www.unicef.org/sowc/archive/ENGLISH/ The%20State%20of%20the%20World%27s%20Children%20 1987.pdf.

———. "The State of the World's Children 2004: Girls, Education and Development." Available online at http://www. unicef.org/sowc/archive/ENGLISH/The%20State%20of%20t he%20World%27s%20Children%202004.pdf.

———. "The State of the World's Children 2008: Child Survival." Available online at http://www.unicef.org/sowc08/ docs/sowc08.pdf.

"Unite for Children, Unite Against AIDS, the Global Campaign on Children and AIDS," UNICEF. Module 1 Introduction to HIV/AIDS. Available online at http://www.uniteforchildren. org/knowmore/files/Module_1PM.pdf.

"Violence Against Children," UNICEF. Available online at http://www.unicef.org/protection/index_violence.html.

"Voices of Youth: Be in the Know," UNICEF. Available online at http://www.unicef.org/voy/explore/rights/explore_148.html.

"Voices of Youth," UNICEF. Ogechi (17, Nigeria). Available online at http://www.unicef.org/voy/speakout/speakout_ 949.html.

Wang-Breal, Stephanie. "Child-friendly Schools Help Young Rwandans Rediscover Childhood," UNICEF. Available online at http://www.unicef.org/girlseducation/Rwanda_44730.html.

"Water, Environment and Sanitation," UNICEF. Available online at http://www.unicef.org/wes/index.html.

"Youthvoice Quiz," UNICEF. Available online at http://www.unicef.org.uk/youthvoice/personalityquiz.asp?quiz=2.

"18 Candles: The Convention on the Rights of the Child Reaches Majority," *Institut international des droits de l'enfant (IDE)*, 2005. Available online at http://www.ohchr.org/Documents/Publications/crc18.pdf.

Beah, Ishmael. *A Long Way Gone: Memoirs of a Boy Soldier*. New York: Sarah Crichton Books, 2007.

Bookmiller, Kirsten Nakjavani, *The United Nations*. New York: Chelsea House, 2008.

Grahame, Deborah A., *UNICEF*. Milwaukee, WI: World Almanac Library, 2003.

Landau, Elaine. *Your Legal Rights*. New York: Walker and Co., 1995.

Maddocks, Steven. *UNICEF*. Chicago, Ill.: Worldwatch, 2004.

Prior, Katherine. *UNICEF*. London, UK: Franklin Watts, 2001.

Smith, Roger. *UNICEF and Other Human Rights Efforts*. Broomall, Pa.: Mason Crest Publishers, 2007.

UNICEF. *"For Every Child: The UN Convention on the Rights of the Child in Words and Pictures."* New York: Phyllis Fogelman Books, 2001. Foreword by Archbishop Desmond M. Tutu.

WEB SITES

Child Rights Information Network
http://www.crin.org/

CRIN is a global network that coordinates and promotes information on child rights. It distributes news and reports, lobbies, enables advocacy, and promotes knowledge-sharing and coordination among international child rights coalitions and advocacy groups.

Committee on the Rights of the Child
http://www2.ohchr.org/english/bodies/crc/

A body of independent experts that monitors implementation of the United Nations Convention of the Rights of the Child.

UNICEF
http://www.unicef.org/

UNICEF: Unite for Children, Unite against AIDS
http://www.uniteforchildren.org/

Campaign to halt and reverse the spread of the disease by 2015.

United Nations Girls' Education Initiative
http://www.ungei.org/

Campaign to narrow the gender gap in primary and secondary education and to ensure that by 2015 all children complete primary schooling.

UN Millennium Project
http://www.unmillenniumproject.org/

A concrete plan for the world to achieve the Millennium Development Goals (see http: unmillenniumproject.org/goals/index.htm) and to reverse the grinding poverty, hunger, and diseases that affect billions of people.

PICTURE CREDITS

INDEX

ABOUT THE CONTRIBUTORS

ADA VERLOREN is an attorney who teaches in the Center for Afro-American and African Studies (CAAS) at the University of Michigan. She was previously affiliated with the Center for Civil and Human Rights at the University of Notre Dame Law School. She has a Ph.D. in law from the University of London, an LL.M. in international human rights law from the University of Notre Dame, and a law degree from the University of South Africa.

Series editor **PEGGY KAHN** is professor of political science at the University of Michigan-Flint. She teaches courses in European politics, lived in England for many years, and has written about British politics. She has been a social studies volunteer in the Ann Arbor public schools. Her Ph.D. in political science is from the University of California, Berkeley, and her B.A. in history and government is from Oberlin College.